LOVESICK
BLUES

PAUL HEMPHILL

LOVESICK BLUES

The Life of

HANK WILLIAMS

SECKER & WARBURG
LONDON

Published by Secker & Warburg 2005

First published in the United States in 2005 by Viking

2 4 6 8 10 9 7 5 3 1

First published in Great Britain in 2005 by
Secker & Warburg
Random House, 20 Vauxhall Bridge Road,
London SW1V 2SA

Random House Australia (Pty) Limited
20 Alfred Street, Milsons Point, Sydney,
New South Wales 2061, Australia

Random House New Zealand Limited
18 Poland Road, Glenfield,
Auckland 10, New Zealand

Random House (Pty) Limited
Endulini, 5A Jubilee Road, Parktown 2193, South Africa

The Random House Group Limited Reg. No. 954009
www.randomhouse.co.uk

A CIP catalogue record for this book
is available from the British Library

ISBN 0436206404

Printed and bound in Great Britain by
Mackays of Chatham plc, Chatham, Kent

In memory of Marshall Frady

CONTENTS

Hear that lonesome whippoorwill,
He sounds too blue to fly;
That midnight train is whining low,
I'm so lonesome I could cry . . .

—HANK WILLIAMS

LOVESICK
BLUES

Prologue: Summer of '49

On Friday afternoons, he would suddenly loom like a ghost at the top of the hill above our house in Birmingham, announcing his arrival with a long blast on the air horns, hovering there long enough to shift into his lowest gear, then grandly descending for a triumphal victory lap in the dusty red Dodge truck while we kids in the bottoms ceased our ball-playing to gawk as he eased the rig to a shuddering stop at the curb. Those clamorous homecomings never failed to draw a gaggle of neighborhood boys whose own fathers were mere clerks or salesmen, and it went without saying that my daddy and his mighty steed represented something a son could sink his teeth into. "How-*dee*," he would chirp as he dismounted—Minnie Pearl at the Opry—"I'm just so proud to be *hyar*." After a hug for my little sister, a handshake for me, and a kiss for Mama, he was in the living room before we knew it, seated at the black upright piano, winding down the best way he knew: a self-taught honky-tonk man tinkling his way through Hoagy Carmichael's greatest hits. My hero, the King of the Road, was home from the wars.

Over supper, as we dug into pork chops and corn bread and the trimmings, he held forth with tales from the road, a born liar refining his art: "I seen this waitress that had a face so ugly it'd already wore out two bodies. . . . They got watermelons in Texas that grow so fast, the bottoms wear off before you can pick 'em. . . . The 'boys' [state troopers and weigh-station cops] don't take their work near as serious as your daddy does. . . ." He spoke of full moons in the Blue Ridge, of overtaking Greyhounds, of dodging deer caught in the headlights, of wrecks on the highway, of violent thunderstorms and insufferable heat and fog so thick he had to "get out and *feel* the signs." He was a lanky, garrulous east Tennessee hillbilly by birth whose passions were country music and baseball, pinto beans and peach cobbler, thick black coffee and cheap cigars, his wife and two children, and finding what lurked beyond the next curve in the road. Of my adolescent yearnings, my most desperate was that one day I would be invited to ride along and see what all the fuss was about.

That day finally arrived on a Sunday afternoon in August of 1949, when I had turned thirteen. At dusk, as the cicadas cranked up their late-summer serenades, I found myself swinging up into the wide seat of the cab while Daddy walked around the rig to make what amounted to his final preflight inspection of the tires, the lights, the brakes, the air hoses, the mirrors, the gas and oil and water levels. The cavernous trailer had been loaded with huge spools of cotton twine, headed for the tire plants in Cumberland, Maryland, due for delivery at first light Tuesday morning. The interior of the cab was cluttered with the things we would need: ditty bags for our clothes, pillows and blankets, road maps, a tool kit, flares, a flashlight, dirty rags, oil cans, kitchen matches and spare cigars, Mama's roast beef sandwiches wrapped in wax paper, a thermos of coffee. Dangling from the dashboard was a radio, whose importance I would discover in due time. As I settled deeper into the shotgun perch that would be my home for the next five days and nights, I discovered something that might become problematic for a boy my age during the 1,500 miles of jostling that lay ahead: taped to the ceiling of the cab, smiling back at me and wearing just about nothing, there was Rita Hayworth in her famous cheesecake photograph.

Mama leaned in for a last good-bye. "Now, Paul," she said, "I don't want him to come back wanting to be a truck driver."

"It's good enough for me," he said, "and I notice there ain't nobody starvin'."

Ignition, contact. *Vroom, vroom, vroom.* With a roar of the engine and a farewell burp on the air horns, we eased away from the house. And then we were gone, father and son, off on the great adventure.

Those were simpler times in America. The roadways were narrow two-lane asphalt, long before anyone had designed a high-speed interstate system. The trucks were rudimentary, a step up from farm machinery—no power steering, no power brakes, no air-conditioning, no sleeper cabs with king-size beds and stand-up showers, no citizens band radios—and under these conditions Daddy had to run a gauntlet fraught with logging trucks, drunks in pickups, cops hiding behind billboards, and women driving half a mile to the grocery store in the family sedan. He was not a company driver on salary but rather a "leased operator," a freelance driver counting on net profit, which meant taking catnaps in the cab rather than checking in to motels; nibbling on snacks from home rather than loading up on meals at truck stops; placing collect calls to the house to speak to himself as a means of letting Mama know of his progress ("Just tell Hemp I'll try again from Bluefield, about noon tomorrow"). The tire companies didn't care how he did it; just deliver the stuff on time.

Anything beyond Chattanooga was new to me, a wide-eyed

kid seeing the world through the bug-spattered windshield of his father's truck, and by ten o'clock we were rolling into the hills of east Tennessee toward Knoxville and Bristol. This was lonesome business, I could see, and without the radio it would have been downright tedious. It was a Motorola, jury-rigged to the dashboard by wires, and through it I was being hurled into a magical realm I had never heard before. Sure, we often picked up WSM out of Nashville to hear the Grand Ole Opry wavering in and out on Saturday nights at home, but what we were hearing now was exotic stuff. Here came XERF, an outlaw station in Ciudad Acuna, Mexico, booming up from the Rio Grande with 500,000 watts, enough power to blow away any local station between Texas and the North Pole, with a mixture of country music and earnest pitches for "magic prayer cloths" and oil-on-velvet paintings of *The Last Supper* and "one thousand baby chicks, folks, sex not guaranteed, for as long as He makes this offer possible," everything short of autographed photographs of Jesus himself. Here came WHO from Des Moines, and WWVA out of Wheeling, and a half dozen others, all fighting for space on the airwaves as we rocked along the mountainous roads, the wind in our hair, listening to the all-night truckers' shows to stay awake.

Daddy's favorite was WCKY out of Cincinnati, 50,000 watts reaching "forty-eight states plus Canada, Cuba, Mexico, and all the ships at sea." These pronouncements came from Nelson King, the voice of country music, who had just kicked off the late-night "Hillbilly Jamboree" with a trademark theme song, "Steel Guitar Rag," which had the twanging upbeat rhythm of a tractor-trailer rig shifting into overdrive. "And now," King said after a tire commercial, "here comes that lovesick boy. . . ." The disc jockeys weren't even bothering anymore to say it was "this newcomer Hank Williams" whose "Lovesick Blues" was riding at the top of the charts. Daddy leaned over to turn up the volume so we could hear the pained yodel and the whining steel guitar that echoed his nasal wail. Hank sang like a hurt animal. They were the loneliest sounds we had ever heard.

> *I got a feeling called the blues, oh, Lord,*
> *Since my baby said good-bye,*
> *Lord, I don't know what I'll do-ooo-ooo*
> *All I do is sit and sigh-ee-yi-ee-yi-yiii . . .*

Startled, Daddy twirled his cigar. "Good *Lord*!"

"Boy," I said, "he's pretty good, ain't he?"

" 'Good'? I ain't never heard anything like it."

We had heard him before, of course, singing "Lovesick Blues" on the Opry broadcasts, but he had never sounded quite like this. Hank Williams's songs were cries from the darkness; made to be heard, it seemed to us, while running through the lonely night, racing with the moon, the wind whistling through the cab, gliding past See Rock City barns and Burma Shave signs and spooky pastures milling with dumbstruck cows. With the whining of the tires keeping time, we laughed at each other's attempts to emulate Hank's yodel.

Strung out along the highways like oases were the truck stops, their blinking neon lights invitations to come in from the dark, pull up a stool, take a load off. Bud's Truck Rest. Thelma's Eats. Dew Drop Inn. Outside: gravel parking lots the size of football fields, bristling with big rigs bearing Confederate-flag bug screens and fanciful monikers like *Lady Luck* and *Long*

Gone Daddy. Inside: bacon and eggs, grits and biscuits, endless refills of coffee from steaming silver urns; truckers at the counters and in the booths and at the Formica tables, some dazed and jittery from the NoDoz and "bennies" keeping them awake; insolent waitresses named Mae and Ruby; a pulsating jukebox offering nothing but the twangy heartfelt country music of Ernest Tubb and Hank Snow and Webb Pierce and now, in this summer of his coming out, Hank Williams. No "Mairzy Doats" here.

"Would you look what the cat drug in. How you doin', Paul?"

"Fair to partly cloudy, Mae."

"That your boy? Looks just like you."

"Well, he can't help it," Daddy said.

For me, the kid sitting on a bar stool, eating lemon icebox pie and washing it down with a glass of milk at two o'clock in the morning somewhere on the ragged fringes of civilization, it was an abrupt baptism into a larger world: a brotherhood of grown-ups making it through the night, wrestling with the lonesomes, dancing with the blues, wisecracking their way toward another sunrise that might bring a better day. In one of the booths, set against wide windows streaked with sweat, some trucker must have punched every Hank Williams song on the amazing technicolor jukebox because here came everything this self-taught Alabama country boy had to offer: not only "Lovesick" but "Lost Highway" and "Mind Your Own Business" and all the other lamentations he had been able to articulate at this point in his life. Here was "Move It on Over," about a husband sharing accommodations in the doghouse; "Wedding Bells," the tale of a jilted boyfriend; and "Mansion on the Hill," about a poor boy's losing the heart of a girl who

figured rich was better. Shouted over the roar of the jukebox
and the whirring of the floor fans, the tit-for-tat continued, un-
abated, with musical rhythms of its own:

— *You want grits with them eggs, hon?*
— *Just a few.*
— *Lookie here, Mae, I got me a bad case of the lovesick*
  blues.
— *Take another one o' them bennies, you'll get over it.*
— *How come you're so damn mean?*
— *You oughta see my husband.*
— *No, thanks.*
— *Where you headed, Tex?*
— *Hell, far as I can figure.*

The years following the Second World War represent the
golden age of country music, written and performed by southern boys and girls not a day's bus ride from the cotton fields or
Appalachian hollows whence they had come. Except for the
complicated rhythms of Bob Wills and His Texas Playboys, a
cowboy's version of the danceable swing of the time, there was
nothing fancy about it. All you needed was a stand-up bass
and a rhythm guitar to set the beat, a jaunty fiddle, a crying
steel guitar, and a singer with an ache in his voice. The lyrics
dealt not with true love and harvest moons and life as it should
be, but rather with the way it had turned out: broken hearts,
dead mamas, whiskey, knife fights, prison, graveyards, unrequited love, loneliness. To people in cities like Chicago and
New York, especially the more sophisticated songwriters on
Tin Pan Alley, country music was for losers. But for people
like my father it was the latest news from home. On another
trip, at another time, upon hearing a dirge about a soldier in

Korea getting "A Dear John Letter" from his girlfriend ("for my love for you has died like the grass upon the lawn"), he shook his head as though he had just heard it on the evening news: "Hell of a thing to do to some old boy, ain't it?" It was music by the folks, for the folks, and the true believers in an audience that sprawled all the way from the Clinch Mountains in Virginia to El Paso in west Texas couldn't care less what anybody else thought.

Hank Williams had come to us from out of nowhere—sprouting like a wild dandelion in the dank forests of south Alabama, some primordial beast who had been let loose on the land, a specimen heretofore undiscovered—and by this summer of '49 nobody seemed to know exactly what to make of him. Only two months after his debut on the Opry with "Lovesick Blues," a startling performance raucously received at old Ryman Auditorium in downtown Nashville, a converted tabernacle referred to as the Mother Church of Country Music, he had suddenly become the best of the best in the best of all times. Born sickly, half-educated, virtually fatherless, an alcoholic by his teen years, untutored musically, unlucky in love at every turn, he had somehow emerged as a tortured genius, a raw poet, the "hillbilly Shakespeare," a Vincent van Gogh of the southern outback. The more traumatic his personal life got, the better he became as a songwriter. To some, it was like looking at a bad wreck. If he wasn't America's greatest songwriter, then certainly he was its most enigmatic.

During those glimmering days and nights of our odyssey into the southern Appalachians, Daddy and I knew little of that. We certainly had no inkling that the man who was singing to us over the truck radio would be dead of whiskey and despair in less than four years, at the age of twenty-nine.

All we knew then was that he seemed to be living his life and writing his songs for *us*, an Alabama trucker and his young son, and that was all that mattered. It was as though he had opened our mail, eavesdropped on our dreams, felt our pulses, found the key to our souls. He was following us everywhere we went, mile for mile, turn for turn, as we chugged upward to reach narrow moonlit mountain passes and then swooped down like a hawk through broad valleys glistening with morning dew, the sound of his voice like a mournful overture for a movie that was certain to end in disaster. More than half a century later, he speaks to me still—*Did you ever see a robin weep . . . I'll never get out of this world alive . . . You'll cry and cry, and try to sleep . . . I'm so lonesome I could cry*—and it's uncanny how those words have stayed with me, in my life and in my work, as they stayed with my father until he died.

The trip went without incident. We dropped the spools of twine at daybreak on that Tuesday, ran empty to pick up a load of finished tires at a factory in Akron, Ohio, then turned south for the return to Birmingham. There were more days and nights of the same—catnaps in the cab, late-night snacks at truck stops, my furtive glances to see if Rita Hayworth had winked, more XERF and WCKY, "Hillbilly Jamboree" and "Lovesick Blues"—until finally, on Friday afternoon, the weary travelers poised on the hill above the house before slowly descending to the bottoms. This time it was I who was swarmed by the boys in the neighborhood, wanting to know how it had gone Out There. I assured Mama that truck-driving looked to me like a lot of hard work. Daddy, meanwhile, had slipped into the house and gone straight to the piano. He had suddenly dropped Hoagy Carmichael from his repertoire and gone directly to Hank

Williams. And that was only the beginning. Over the ensuing decades our lives would imitate Hank's art well beyond his death. In the best of our times, and most especially in the worst, Hank Williams was always with us. He simply would not go away.

Young Hiram

Not unlike the boy who would become its most famous son, the south Alabama of the 1930s was lean and hungry, untamed, isolated from mainstream America, and desperate to find a way out of the wilderness. The stark black-and-white photographs of *Let Us Now Praise Famous Men,* a book documenting life in rural central Alabama during the Depression, could just as well have been taken in Butler County, about a hundred miles to the south. Smack in the middle of the Black Belt, named for the rich black soil that once nourished cotton in profusion, the land had been in steady decline since the end of the Civil War, which had cost the cotton barons their free workforce and their plantations and finally their spirit. On the square in the town of Enterprise, they had erected a statue "honoring" the boll weevil, the nasty little critter that had all but wiped out cotton, thereby steering Alabama away from its tenuous one-industry economy. Now it had become mean country—sparse, exposed to the elements, virtually cashless— where it was every man for himself in the daily search for the next meal, a smile, an entertainment, some hope, *anything.* Out there in the dense forests of pines and hardwoods, sharing space with wild animals in a world apart from the small towns that had sprung up along the railroad lines, the people traveled by mule, built their own houses, made their clothes, grew their vegetables, hunted and fished not for sport but for the food.

They were as one with nature, riding out summer thunder-storms of downright biblical proportions. They knew the terrifying scream of the panther in the night, the wail of a mother whose child had died at birth, the cries of hungry children weakened by pellagra and hookworm, the sighing of wind through the pines, the mocking call of a whistle from a train headed for somewhere else. From their outposts in the woods—a log cabin with an outhouse, a well, and a pea patch—they could only try to ride it out with the help of a Lord who didn't seem to have much of a sense of humor.

Among them was Alonzo Huble Williams, whose family had drifted in from North Carolina during Reconstruction. Having lost his mother to suicide when he was six and his father to a vague "fever" when he was a teenager, Lon Williams had spent most of his life as a lost child in scattered lumber-company encampments in the deep woods—as a gofer, a water boy, an ox driver, whatever was needed—while the burly older men spent long days driving off the poisonous snakes and working their two-man band saws. He was there when the tracks were laid for the new Gulf, Florida & Alabama Railroad, among the men who drolly noted that GF&A actually stood for "gophers, frogs, and alligators." Since the few salaried jobs in those parts were with the lumber companies and the railroads, vigorously plundering the South's virgin forests, he didn't dare complain. In his adulthood he found himself assigned to the log trains that ran on narrow-gauge tracks, hauling away the trees as they were felled, and this was about as good as it could get. He felt he was on his way. Thus emboldened, he proposed marriage to a big-boned teenaged girl named Jessie Lillybelle Skipper, who lived with her sprawling family in a logging community called Chapman, and at the end of 1916 they became Lon and Lillie Williams. If they seemed an odd couple from the beginning, this laconic twenty-five-year-old and his high-strung eighteen-year-old bride, the worst was yet to come.

Little more than a year after the wedding, Lon found himself in France, attached to a U.S. Army division in the waning days of the First World War, fighting not the chemical warfare and constant bombardment by the Germans but a fellow soldier over a French woman. He got hit in the face with a wine bottle and was kicked in the head while down, spent a week in a hospital, and was promptly sent back to the front lines. The war was about over, anyway, and after less than a year of service he was back home in the summer of 1919, driving log trains again, as though nothing had happened. Lillie had stayed with her family while he was gone, and upon Lon's return they resumed the nomadic life of the logger: following the "crop," as it were, living in abandoned houses or converted boxcars or with other logging couples all over that corner of the state.

When their only son was born, Lillie and Lon were living on a dirt road a few miles outside the little town of Georgiana in a settlement known as West Mount Olive. Their abode was a double-pen log cabin bisected by a dogtrot—a breezeway separating the three-room living area from a country store, whence they sold vegetables and the strawberries harvested from a large patch beside the house. Lillie had given birth to a child who died in infancy, then to a healthy daughter named Irene, and they were getting by well enough with Lon's salary and the meager proceeds from the strawberry operation, when she went into labor again. This time, at least, they could summon a doctor by phone, an amenity a man could brag about in those

days, and on September 17, 1923, the doctor and a black mid-
wife brought forth a boy. They named him Hiram, after the biblical King Hiram of Tyre, although when they got around to
registering the birth it was recorded as "Hiriam." That didn't
matter much, anyway. He would be known to all as "Harm," in
the southern country pronunciation, until he took matters into
his own hands as a teenager and adopted the name he fancied
most: Hank. Hank Williams.

Problems abounded. He was a scrawny kid born with a de-
formity in the spinal column, a failure of the vertebrae to fuse
properly, leaving a raised spot on his spine. This was worri-
some to the parents, something they could only hope would
work itself out, nobody knowing at the time that it was spina
bifida occulta, curable if caught early, but potentially crippling
if left to fester. And that wasn't all. After seven years, the marriage was turning out to be a union from hell. Lillie, never
dainty, had ballooned to lumberman proportions: well over two
hundred pounds and nearly six feet tall, given to draping herself in tent-sized dresses, a fierce sight with her heaving bosom
and mass of black hair and arched eyebrows, the sort of woman
who, as the men were wont to say, "don't take no shit from nobody." Poor Lon, three or four inches shorter than his bride, almost dapper with his beady brown eyes and narrow lips, just
wanted to get along. He drove his trains through the woods all
day and then came home to play with the two kids, pamper his
strawberries, sip his moonshine, and roll his cigarettes. He
had learned to stay out of the way when Lillie went off on her
tirades about shiftless men in perilous times.

Well, Lillie and her in-laws would say in her defense, somebody had to wear the pants in the family. A frost that killed the
strawberries prompted more moves, one to a converted boxcar

in a lumber camp, and just about the time Lon had bought a house on ten acres in McWilliams, where he had spent much of his own childhood, he was revisited by the wounds suffered during his beating in France. He began feeling paralysis in the face, forcing him to take on a series of lighter jobs with various lumber outfits until, finally, he was unable to work at all. Lillie managed to deliver him to the Veterans Administration hospital in Pensacola, on Florida's gulf coast, in 1930, and before he knew it he was being diagnosed with a brain aneurysm and being admitted to a VA hospital four hundred miles away from home in Alexandria, Louisiana. Young Hiram was six when Lon left, getting his first taste of formal education in the woeful one-room schoolhouses in the countryside, and never again would he know what it was like to have his father around the house. Some years later, as a lonesome teenager, he would scribble a piece of doggerel entitled "I Wish I Had a Dad," on how it might have been: *The dad I've got, you see, he comes but once a year / I ask him why he stayed away and he said lookie here, and tried to take my mind away by pulling at my ear / Mom wasn't there, she never is when Papa pays a call / When she came back I tried to talk, but Mom said that's all. . . .* The fact is, the boy wouldn't see his father again for nearly ten years.

Lon was history, as far as Lillie was concerned. Early in 1931, when it had become official that America was in a Depression, she and the kids left the country for good and moved into a house in Georgiana. People could talk all they wanted to about Lillie's abrasive personality—and talk they did, about just what kind of a deal she had made with the rich bachelor, one Thaddeus B. Rose, who gave her the house, rent-free, so she could open it up to boarders—but she was determined to make a better life for Irene and Hiram and herself. Georgiana, with a population of about two thousand, was a lively railroad town, a retail trading center serving as a magnet for all the surrounding communities, with names like Garland, McKenzie, Avant, Chapman, and Bolling. Everything centered on the Louisville & Nashville Railroad depot, where some two dozen freights and seven passenger trains stopped each day. There were cotton warehouses, a gin, livery stables, blacksmiths, and all of the attendant services: groceries, a dozen hotels and rooming houses, eateries, a mercantile store. There was even a twenty-four-hour barbershop with complete amenities—haircuts, shaves, shoe shines, showers—not only for the rail travelers but for the farmers as well: men who would move their ox-drawn wagons into line at the cotton gin, one of eight throughout Butler County; often faced with an overnight stay, they had plenty of spare time to get themselves preened, catch up on the news, swap stories, sip some whiskey, and inevitably get into trouble.

Lillie's place was four blocks from the depot, on Rose Street, beside the tracks as they entered town, headed south toward the ports at Mobile and New Orleans. It was an airy wooden structure raised six feet off the ground on stilts, a design Thaddeus Rose had brought from his previous life in the swamplands of Mississippi and Louisiana, with an outhouse and a single spigot for water and an open fireplace for cooking. She got busy making the best of what she had—stuffing corn shucks into feed sacks for mattresses, fashioning furniture from apple crates, accepting anything her neighbors had to offer—and did quite well for herself and the kids. Lack of cash was the problem for everyone in those days, even though a loaf of bread cost only four cents, and she alleviated that somewhat by taking in boarders, serving as the night nurse at a nearby hospital, working at a cannery, and sending the kids out on the streets to sell peanuts and sandwiches. And in due time, through the help of Lister Hill, a man embarking on a long career as an Alabama politician, she began collecting the departed Lon's full military disability pension. This was a time for entrepreneurs, people with ideas and the energy to pull them off. There was a Czech in town named Pete Wolf, who oversaw the toppling of rare white oaks out in the forests, trimmed and bundled them, and then had them shipped to Europe to be fashioned into staves for barrels used in the aging of wine. Another man, Newt Rhodes, discovered a market in Mobile for the chickens he raised and put on the freight in crates. Lillie, as energetic as any man, brusque as a warden, had found her calling as a boardinghouse operator—some would say, unkindly, a madam—in a town throbbing with people just passing through.

For young Hiram, fresh in from the country, this was like living in a toy store. A whole new world had opened up for him and he was gulping it in; an adventuresome barefoot boy on a bicycle, with people to meet, places to go, and things to explore. As soon as school let out each day, he was on his way downtown to see what was up. Unattended urchins roamed the streets in the afternoons, sniffing and poking around like kittens in strange new surroundings, and there was much to see. Henry Ford's first automobiles had begun to appear in Georgiana, so there were those blatting wheeled monsters to be investigated; and Bunk Blackmon's blacksmith shop; and "niggertown," on the other side of the L&N tracks, where the kin of freed slaves lived crowded together in their hovels; and diners where people actually sat down and ordered their meals; and Jim Warren's music store, holding an array of gleaming new guitars and fiddles; and the train depot itself. For a kid with wheels and orders from his mother to get out and hustle up some cash, the possibilities were endless. He sold peanuts and fruit and sandwiches, shined shoes, delivered newspapers and groceries, and was generally available to run errands of any sort.

More to the point, the boy who would become Hank Williams was learning the fine art of ingratiating himself, of convincing people that they absolutely had to have his services; an imperative for someone in show business. The way to avoid the wrath of Lillie Williams was to do what she said, to kowtow with a smile, and that was the way to sell a bag of peanuts or a shoe shine to a stranger on the street as well. It doesn't seem too much of a stretch to say that he was learning these elemental lessons in entertainment, as it were, as a small boy just trying to survive, and most likely his musical education got a jump start in the fall of 1933, as he was turning ten, when he was temporarily shipped out to live with relatives fifty miles west of Georgiana in a lumber community called Fountain. It was a simple swap—Hiram for his teenaged cousin, Opal McNeil, who would live with Lillie in Georgiana, where there was a high school she could attend—and the transaction sent the boy packing again for the country. He moved in with his aunt and uncle, Walter and Alice McNeil, in an L-shaped "house" composed of two converted boxcars (Uncle Walter drove a log train for a lumber outfit), was enrolled in a one-room school, and for at least that one school year enjoyed a normal family life.

Given the financial struggles and the caterwauling that had

raged between strong-willed Lillie and the ever-weakening Lon before he left, Hiram had spent his first go-around in the deep woods lying low and trying to stay out of the way. His first taste of music had come at his mother's knee, literally, as he perched on a stool beside her on Sunday mornings, lustily joining in the singing while Lillie played the organ and bellowed from the hymnal at the hard-shell Baptist church in West Mount Olive. Thrilled that the boy's interest in music might be used to celebrate the Lord, she had bought him a Sears Silvertone guitar when he was eight and even enrolled him in a church singing school. There was no radio at the big house on Rose Street, but he had heard his share of recorded music at the music store and the diners and the other commercial establishments in Georgiana, where the strains of gospel tunes and the earliest country recordings drifted through the open windows. The arrival of the raucous roadhouses on the edge of town, the dangerous "fightin'-'n'-dancin' clubs" where Hank Williams would serve his apprenticeship, was still a couple of years away.

But young "Harm" found simple southern music at its source during his sojourn in Fountain. Little churches were everywhere in the countryside of Monroe County (scant miles from where a young woman named Nelle Harper Lee would write the novel *To Kill a Mockingbird*), sanctuaries for both the Scots-Irish lumber people and the freed African American slaves now toiling as sharecroppers and tenant farmers in what remained of the cotton fields. This time around, with no whip-cracking mother to stay on his case, the kid had a pal his age as a running mate, his cousin J. C. McNeil. The boys ran free in the woods—fishing, hunting, eavesdropping through the windows of the primitive white *and* black churches to hear the pained yowls of gloom and doom ("Sadly we sing and with tremulous breath . . . In the valley and by the dark river of death . . .")—and on Saturday nights they hovered around the edges of the roiling country dances held in schoolhouses beneath the pines. Things may have been different in certain other parts of the South, where the fiercest Pentecostal churches held such sway that they wouldn't allow dancing, on the grounds that any expressions of joy would have to be deferred until the afterlife. But here, when the week's drudgery was over, it was time for the men to find some booze, grab a fiddle, kick up their heels, and take their ladies dancing. Those places could turn into bloodbaths, passions being stirred by the volatile mixture of whiskey and live music, and the two young cousins on the sidelines found their own way to join right in. It was simple, really. Since Baptists, as the saying goes even today, "don't like to drink in front of each other," Hiram and J. C. watched to see where the men stashed their whiskey outside in the bushes, out of deference to the Lord and to their wives, and helped themselves when the grown-ups went back inside. The boys would be laid out stone-cold drunk in the woods before they knew what had hit them. This was the beginning of Hank Williams's drinking, the curse of his life, and its pattern was set early on: booze made him feel good, helped him to forget his troubles, and if he came across a bottle he couldn't give it up until it was empty.

If at first it seemed the boy had simply been away at camp for a year, when he returned to Georgiana that summer it was clear that he had undergone vast changes. There had been his discovery of booze as an escape, of course; and learning the basic chords on the guitar from his aunt Alice; and experiencing the joys and sorrows of the heartfelt backwoods music in the churches and at the dances. And there was much more. It would be hard to argue that the sensitive Hiram, a quick learner who took every experience to heart, hadn't filed away the observations that later would be hailed as some of his greatest lines as a songwriter: a robin weeping as the leaves begin to fall, having "lost the will to live"; a moon going behind a cloud "to hide its face and cry"; the "silence of a falling star" lighting up a purple sky. Rather than relying on secondary sources—commercial radio, tape recordings, songwriting lessons—he had gone straight to the roots: alone, in the woods, making mental notes of what he saw and heard and felt. Back in town, a frail kid who had seen enough of the bruising life of men whose lot was to cut down trees and drag them away, he seemed to have found an option even as he approached his eleventh birthday. He would make music.

About thirty percent of the people living in Georgiana during the Depression were African American, descendants of the slaves whose sweat had made cotton king before the Civil War, and those six hundred or so souls had learned to keep a low profile. Although the Ku Klux Klan was a raging force throughout the deep South and even in the Midwest in those days, night-riding Klansmen were seldom seen in Butler County. The unspoken "Jim Crow" laws separating the races had sufficiently cowed the blacks to the point of utter submission. (When the big store in town, Morgan's, raffled off a new Ford T-Model in the early thirties, the winning ticket turned out to belong to a black man. Dead certain of what would happen if he accepted the car—*A nigger! Riding around town in a brand-new automobile!*—the winner chose to take the cash instead, about $300, more than enough for a train ticket to get the hell out of there.) The black folks in town knew their place, all right, which was as domestics or as "snake men" paid to clear the woods of rattlers and copperheads in advance of the timber crews. If they wanted to entertain the white folks, now, that was quite another matter.

Thus, Hiram, back in town for good after his tour of duty in the countryside, must have felt his heart jump up into his throat the first time he saw a sight that was new on the streets of Georgiana: an old black man with a guitar, strumming and singing for passersby, nodding and smiling and mumbling a thank-you whenever someone dropped a coin into the crumpled hat set at his feet. It was the boy's first glimpse of a professional musician at work, if playing for nickels and dimes could be called such, and he attached himself to the man like a leech. His name was Rufus Payne, but everybody knew him as "Tee-Tot," in a wry nod to his drinking. He wasn't a drunk, but he certainly wasn't a teetotaler, at all times packing a flask holding a concoction of moonshine whiskey and tea. He had lived a nomadic life himself, being born on a plantation up around Selma in 1884; living for many years in New Orleans, where his father was a "mule skinner" with a mule and a wagon for hire, and where Rufus had learned the blues and jazz; and now, finally, he was living fifteen miles up the L&N tracks from Georgiana in Greenville, the seat of Butler County. He was about fifty years old, lived somewhat fitfully with a wife who was not amused by his drinking, or his "evil" music, and a son Hiram's age who was born to another woman. He picked up some steady income by working as a janitor and a delivery-man for a drugstore. Mostly, though, he regarded himself as a troubadour. He performed on the streets of Greenville, some-times with one friend on a harmonica and another on a "wash-

tub bass," a thumping contraption consisting of an overturned
galvanized tub and a broomstick and a rope. Now and then, to
reach new audiences, he would get on the train alone and ride
down the tracks to perform at the depot and on the sidewalks
in Georgiana.

Hiram was mesmerized. Tee-Tot had the temerity to dress
as well as he could afford, wearing a jacket and a tie if the
weather was right, hoping to give the appearance that he was a
lot more than just some shiftless old black man begging for a
handout. He sang the blues and threw in some gospel, adding
a lazy effect on his guitar with the use of a slide stuck on a finger of his fretting hand (fashioned from the broken neck of a
whiskey bottle), and he knew how to pitch a song: singing and
strumming with much verve, stooping and bowing, laughing
and crying; a serious performer at work. They became quite a
pair, this skinny eleven-year-old white kid and the aging black
man, moving from the train depot to the busier places like just
outside the entrance of the barbershop or on the sidewalk near
the music store. Hiram had already learned all of the chords
he would need to know from his aunt Alice, and there was
never any evidence that the future Hank Williams ever took
any specific song ideas from Tee-Tot.

What he did take was plenty. He learned the blues, and
how to showcase it, and he couldn't get enough. Hiram followed Tee-Tot everywhere when the old man came to town during that summer of '34, pestering him, offering fifteen cents or
whatever he could come up with to buy his companionship and
maybe a lesson on certain blues notes (and certainly a nip of
whiskey now and then), to such an extent that one time Tee-
Tot, lured to Rose Street by the promise of a meal, warned Lillie that he was afraid white folks might start getting agitated

over the sight of the two of them hanging out together all of the time. Lillie was too busy making a living to be concerned about that, on the one hand, but on the other she was delighted to see that her son had found something he was good at, something that might have a future.

Always looking ahead, to something away from all of this small-town drudgery, Lillie packed up the kids and made what would turn out to be an intermittent move, fifteen miles up the tracks, in the fall of 1934. Greenville was the seat of Butler County, four times larger than Georgiana, with a population of about eight thousand, much more prosperous and, in a relative way, more sophisticated. There she found a large house for rent and opened up another boardinghouse, just off the courthouse square, and enrolled Hiram and Irene in purportedly better schools. By dint of her hard work, plus Lon's pension checks and the pittances brought home by the children, she was doing much better financially now and the future looked more promising. The center of action in Greenville was the county courthouse, not the railroad depot as in Georgiana, meaning an upgrade in clientele: lawyers, politicians, and salesmen in place of red-dirt farmers. This was still the Depression, no way around it, but the accretion of time and the larger playing field meant more of everything: more automobiles, electricity and running water, more playmates for the kids, and a larger pool of possible male companions for a more or less single mother now in her mid-thirties, no matter how demanding and unattractive and downright *mean* she might be.

For Hiram, the world just kept on expanding. Now there was a larger movie theater, where he was a regular at the day-long "pitcher shows" featuring cowboy singing stars every Saturday. Now Lillie had bought her first radio, an old Philco, on which for the first time he could listen regularly to stations like WSFA in Montgomery and even WSM in Nashville, home of the fairly new Grand Ole Opry. Now, of course, there was a much larger marketplace for the peanuts and sandwiches and shoe shines he was still expected to pitch, and for the music he had begun to beggar on the streets just as he had learned from Tee-Tot Payne in Georgiana. School be damned, anyway. Hiram was enrolled, but he wasn't there in spirit, much preferring to spend his time reading comic books, going to the movies, listening to the radio, and making music of his own. He usually took his guitar to school, and it didn't take much prodding from his schoolmates for him to break into the first song anyone remembers his writing: *I had an old goat / She ate tin cans / When the little goats came / They were Ford sedans.*

Even as he approached his teens, he was a shy and introverted kid—gawky, wearing rimless spectacles (for the damage caused by a dose of hookworm he had contracted while going barefoot), sprouting like a weed, ears like barnyard doors—and as it turned out the only good friend he had during those days was, once again, Rufus Payne. Tee-Tot's house was a shack near the railroad tracks in Greenville, and seldom did a day pass when they weren't together: swapping licks at the old man's house, playing for change on the sidewalks, peeking in on the blacks-only gin joints in town, performing on busy Saturdays at the courthouse square, running by Lillie's boardinghouse for something from the kitchen. They shared the blues and they shared nips of whiskey from Tee-Tot's flask, and more than once the boy wound up spending the night at

his old mentor's place, dragging his sad frame home at daybreak to face his mother's wrath—*Just like your no-good
drunken father!*—before changing clothes for school.

Lillie and the kids weren't long for Greenville, which was
proving too small to satisfy her dreams, and it's quite likely
that an event that occurred at Hiram's middle school in the
spring of '37 just about did it for her. On a regular school day,
the seventy-odd boys were going through their routine of calis-
thenics out on the football field behind the school. The field
was encircled by a plank fence separating it from the railroad
tracks. The man in charge of physical-education class was a
brutish former University of Alabama football player who
couldn't abide slackers. Hiram Williams, the skinny kid with
the glasses, was goofing off while everybody else obediently
hut-hutted through their side-straddle hops. The coach came
up behind Hiram and kicked him in the butt, sending him
sprawling into the dust, and when the kid scrambled to his feet
he was cussing a blue streak, enraged, charging the coach like
a bantam rooster. The coach grabbed him by the nape of the
neck, dragged him to the plank fence, ripped off a board, and
proceeded to paddle him in front of his schoolmates. The boy's
tears were more from rage and embarrassment than from pain,
and when he got home that afternoon he certainly told Mama.
Lillie went on the warpath, threatening to take on the coach
herself if the school board didn't fire him, but the story grew
stale in the summer's heat and it went away. Came July, and
the Williams clan was on the move again, this time to a big city
where this sort of thing didn't happen.

The Singing Kid

In July of 1937, while thousands of Okies were bailing out
and heading west for a new start (*Well, I'm goin' to California, where they sleep out every night,* sang Jimmie Rodgers, the
first king of country music, before he died of tuberculosis in
'33), Lillie Williams and the kids were relocating, too, if on a
more modest scale. They would move not halfway across the
nation, only forty miles up the road to Montgomery, the state
capital. Montgomery's population of seventy-five thousand
made it the third-largest city in Alabama, behind gritty steel-making Birmingham and the smelly port of Mobile, and it offered better opportunities for Lillie as a boardinghouse
operator and for the children with its improved schools and
broader entertainments. Enlisting the help of her brother-in-law Walter McNeil, who had moved his brood into town from
Fountain, they lashed their belongings to a makeshift platform
on the back of his logging truck and were delivered to a large
house on South Perry Street, not far from the same statehouse
where Jefferson Davis had been sworn in as president of the
Confederacy. It was around this time that her son announced
that "Hiram" wouldn't cut it anymore. From his exposure to
cowboy movies and country radio shows and comic books, he
had determined that "Hank" was more in line with the career
he fancied for himself, as a writer and singer of country songs.

The newly reconstituted "Hank Williams" grew from boy to man almost overnight. He was expected to continue hitting the streets with his shoe shine kit and bags of peanuts, bringing home cash for the family coffer, but now he saw a dual purpose in that enterprise. WSFA, the radio giant of sparsely populated central Alabama, had its studios on the mezzanine of the Jefferson Davis Hotel, and he instinctively knew to commandeer the sidewalk below the station's windows as his base of operations, where he would sing a little, shine some shoes, sell some peanuts, and sing some more. The Jeff Davis equated with the railroad depot in Georgiana for its centrality—downtown headquarters for traveling salesmen, notorious hangout for rural state legislators in town for some politicking and hoorawing, destination for musicians angling for work on WSFA's many live music shows—and this skinny, bespectacled kid with a guitar had the audacity to insinuate himself in the middle of it all. Soon enough, an engineer was running a line out onto the sidewalk to pick up a remote broadcast of "the Singing Kid" at work, inspiring the boy's proud mama to advise her friends to call the station and demand more, leading the music director to invite him inside to actually sing into a live microphone. Toward the end of that year, as a fourteen-year-old with the singing voice of an adult, Hank entered an amateur talent contest at the Empire Theater with a song he had written, the "WPA Blues"—*I got a home in Montgomery / A place I like to stay / But I have to work for the WPA / And I'm dissatisfied, I'm dissatisfied*—winning the fifteen-dollar prize money and promptly blowing it on booze and other treats for himself and what pals he had. Lillie wasn't pleased about that part, just another reminder that he was his ne'er-do-well father's son, but she nevertheless helped him buy a shiny new

Gibson guitar with a sunburst finish to replace the old Sears Silvertone now showing its age.

When he had won so many of those amateur talent shows that organizers began to dissuade him from entering them, a backward compliment signifying that attention must be paid, Hank found himself in the process of becoming a major player on a small stage. In a blink, it seemed, "the Singing Kid" went from making casual unpaid appearances on a WSFA program featuring a house band to being the star of his own show. Twice a week he appeared on fifteen-minute segments, strumming and singing the country standards of the day, fetching a princely fifteen dollars a week at a time when that was enough money in Depression Alabama to support a couple with two kids. Radio was the ticket for a musician during the thirties, in little Montgomery as well as in such larger markets as Nashville and Chicago, where established on-air "barn dances" stoked bigger things. It was synergy at work, one piece spinning off onto another. You sang and played on the radio, prompting requests for personal appearances, leading to show dates; and then, if things worked out, you published songbooks and finally—*who knows?*—you started making records in a studio. The system was a monster that required constant care and feeding. Little did the fans who had begun phoning and writing WSFA with pleas to see and hear this Hank Williams in person know that he was actually a scrawny teenager who lived in his mother's boardinghouse, had neither a car nor a driver's license, got drunk every chance he could, hated school, and was barely a step beyond being just another fatherless urchin selling peanuts and shining shoes on the sidewalks of downtown Montgomery.

In truth, Hank had already left his childhood far behind, back there in the days when he was chasing rabbits through the woods with his cousin and running errands for his drill-sergeant mother on the dusty streets of Georgiana. By the time he was turning fifteen, a growth spurt having put him close to his full height of six-one, he was practically a grown-up. He had been precocious from the beginning, missing little of what went on around him—the lack of any spark between his parents; his mother's conviction that all men were sorry; the way a beaten old black man such as Tee-Tot could express his joys and sorrows only through a bottle and a song; and, now, how the business of music worked—and it must have been quite a shock to everybody when Lon suddenly appeared on the porch at 114 South Perry Street one day in August of '38. Gone since 1930, Lon had managed to spring himself on a furlough from the VA hospital in Louisiana (not with any help from Lillie, who was as surprised as anyone), and now here he was, more or less testing the possibility that he might be able to take his rightful place in the family fold with his wife and children. It was too late, of course. He didn't need Lillie's clucking reminders to see that time had wrought dramatic changes. He had been replaced at the dining table by a cast of wisecracking male boarders competing for the bossy landlady's favors; his daughter was juggling boyfriends and schoolbooks and a business of her own selling sandwiches to clerks and laborers; the son he had christened Hiram was a blossoming radio star who had gone and changed his name. With nowhere else to go, Lon hung around long enough to officially celebrate Hank's birthday in September—now they seemed less like father and son than uncle and nephew—before skulking back to "serve out my sentence" at the hospital. Young Hiram's plaintive ode "I Wish I Had a Dad" had lost its fervency.

.   .   .

Hank performed alone on his fifteen-minute radio shows, singing to his own guitar accompaniment between reading commercials and shamelessly advertising himself, but if he was going to start playing show dates he would have to form a band. He began with a guitar player and vocalist, a married man seven years his senior, Braxton Schuffert, whose early-morning show on WSFA had been one of young Hiram's favorites during the Greenville years. Every country band at that time included a comic, usually someone who played stand-up bass and was willing to play the fool to the star in routines between songs, and that turned out to be Smith "Hezzy" Adair, a teenaged orphan who happened to be living with the Schufferts. For a fiddler, Hank recruited another older man, Freddy Beach, whose portfolio including working the road with an early western swing band and wandering about the boondocks as an evangelist. Now and then they were lucky enough to flush out somebody from the ragtag group of aspiring young musicians hovering around WSFA who could handle what was, at the time, a strange new instrument of Hawaiian heritage— the electrified steel guitar—with a sliding whine that in later years would be the perfect complement to, and a virtual echo of, the tortured voice of Hank Williams. Thus was born the first edition of the Drifting Cowboys, a name waiting for a band, further homage to Hank's boyhood infatuation with western movies. They rustled up some cheap cowboy hats and boots, bought a new set of tires and a case of oil for Braxton Schuffert's chancy V-8 Ford, and pronounced themselves ready to do business.

Because Hank was still attending school, however lack-adaisically, they had to book their dates around that complication. Weekends, summers, and holidays were the prime times, anyway, and they had no trouble finding work. Mired in the Depression, feeling disconnected, broke, and out of meaningful work, people were desperate for a song and a smile. Hank Williams and the Drifting Cowboys rode in to help, crammed into the little black Ford sedan with a bass fiddle strapped on top, working Montgomery and the small towns within an eighty-mile radius where folks were hearing Hank's radio shows, towns with names like Opp, Fort Deposit, and Grove Hill. They would play at any time, any place—private party or public gathering, it didn't matter as long as they got paid—at barbecues, swimming parties, dances, carnivals, county fairs; in schoolhouses or auditoriums or movie theaters or under big tents. They played them all for nearly two solid years, for a fee or for the usual twenty-five-cent admission, their upcoming arrivals announced over WSFA and by posters slapped on buildings and telephone poles. In order to save money, and to ensure that Hank made it to class the following morning, they always made it back to their own beds in Montgomery every night. There was no way school could hold Hank's attention in the face of all this excitement. When he did show up for classes he was so drained that he was useless. ("You want me to wake him up?" a classmate asked when Hank had fallen asleep in class. "Don't bother," said the teacher. "He's not going to learn anything, anyway.") Hank finally dropped out of Sidney Lanier High School in October of 1939, a month after his sixteenth birthday, having just begun the tenth grade. He was now a full-time professional musician. He never looked back.

Most artists of any genre, whether poets or novelists or performers, have begun their careers by emulating those they most admire. Hank wasn't yet writing his own songs, except for the juvenile "WPA Blues," so at this point he settled for cover-

ing anything recorded by his hero, Roy Acuff, the first big star
of the Grand Ole Opry. Fans who paid for a show by Hank
Williams and the Drifting Cowboys first heard the tune Hank
had adopted as his opening theme song—"Happy Roving
Cowboy," written by a Canadian, recorded by the Sons of the
Pioneers—and then got an earful of Acuff's "The Great Speck-
led Bird" and his bathetic ballads about train wrecks and the
folks back home. Between those tearjerkers and at least one
"sacred" song, equally maudlin but regarded as de rigueur in
the southern Bible Belt, they would hear cornpone comedy ex-
changes between Hank the boss and Hezzy the village idiot:
"You ain't got enough sense to *know* you ain't got no sense."
The kid was good, no doubt about it, slick and earnest before
his time—*But he looks so young!*—and he owed much of it to
Tee-Tot Payne's informal tutorials, those years of selling himself to strangers on the sidewalk, and a tyke's eagerness to
please a whip-cracking mother who couldn't be pleased.

Lillie, in fact, was becoming the ultimate stage mom. Most
single middle-aged mothers would be relieved to be shed of
their parental burdens, ready to make a life of their own before
it was too late, but she saw it differently. Fat, old, and tired before her time, cantankerous and settled into her ways, she
knew the limitations of her attraction to successful men whose
star she might ride. She might as well do it through her son.
Hank's sister, Irene, had taken a fling as manager of the Drifting Cowboys in the beginning, even performing briefly as their
"gal singer," but Lillie soon took over the operation. She
bought herself a station wagon, began booking dates and nego-
tiating fees, and took to driving the band to shows, where she
stood at the door like a bouncer to count the gate so the boys
got their fair cut. Nobody was especially pleased about this

turn of events. "Hell, Aunt Lillie wouldn't even let her own relatives in for free," said J. C. McNeil, Hank's cousin. Stuck in the confines of Lillie's station wagon as she drove over the undulating asphalt roads to their next date, the randy young musicians felt severely constricted: no cussing, no drinking, no farting, no bragging about their amorous conquests. Further ingratiating herself—*And after all I've done for you!*—Lillie charged minimal rent at the boardinghouse for Hezzy Adair and other unattached young men in the revolving cast of Drifting Cowboys. She fancied that she was in charge, and that they owed her. She had found her destiny.

And so the apprenticeship of Hank Williams continued; in stops and starts, with or without his mama, with or without his band. Free of any obligations to hustle back home to make the opening bell at school, Hank put together mini tours or extended engagements whenever he could. He and three of the Cowboys thought they had made the big time when they borrowed Lillie's station wagon and drove a hundred miles to a town near the Georgia line to play three shows at a movie theater, at three, six, and nine o'clock, grossing $100. They felt like desperadoes robbing a bank: ride in, take the money, ride out. (On such occasions, if Hank got drunk or they wheedled more money than Lillie had bargained for, he would caution them, "Don't tell Mama.") They followed that bonanza with a series of shows in south Alabama and the panhandle of Florida for a theater chain. In November of '39 Hank and Hezzy arrived on a Sunday at the Ga-Ana Theater in Georgiana, where young Hiram had seen his first cowboy movies, for an event one of his childhood buddies never forgot: "It was their third stop on a tour of Georgia, Alabama, and Florida, and they rolled up in Hezzy's Ford with his bass fiddle on top. The manager had some peach brandy waiting for 'em, and when they ran out of that they found some home brew. Hank got up and said, 'I love this place,' sang 'WPA Blues' and a couple of others, but he was too drunk to stay on so he sat down. The manager thought it was funny as hell. Lord knows how they finished the tour."

Finish they did, landing Hank at the front door of another man who would serve him as both a mentor and an enabler over the years. Pappy Neal McCormick had his own show on WCOA radio, whose giant antenna sprouted from the roof of the ornate San Carlos Hotel in Pensacola, on the western end of Florida's panhandle. Seven stories high, sparkling beside the waters of the Gulf of Mexico, the San Carlos was the center of what action there was in Pensacola: the best accommodations around, surrounded by banks and movie theaters and department stores. Pappy, a Creek Indian who had moved to the coast from rural south Alabama, had developed a large following as leader of the Hawaiian Troubadours, who played for dances every night at the hotel's gaudy ballroom on the second floor. When Hank and Hezzy worked the club that night, the last stop of their three-state tour, it amounted to an audition. Pappy had no need for Hezzy, but he took a shine to Hank and let him know he was welcome any time he was in the area. Hank was smitten by Pappy on two counts: the older man was a dazzling showman, and he was doing things the kid had never heard with the steel guitar. Pappy's, in fact, was a marvel: four guitars in one, really, electrified strings on each side of a block of wood that turned on a barbecue spit. He played it more like a Hawaiian instrument emulating soft Pacific breezes than as a complement to country music (like most

other early steel players, he avidly tuned in to a musical program, "Hawaii Calls," on his shortwave radio). The layover
would lead to a long friendship between the two. Whenever
Lillie's carping got to be too much for Hank to bear, he always
knew he could vanish to Pensacola to make some music with
Pappy, hole up with a bottle at the San Carlos, or both.

Then, to top off Hank's basic education, he encountered
the roadhouses, the "fightin'-'n'-dancin' clubs." They littered
the countryside all over America, but the ones in the rural
South, from the Appalachian hollows to the scruffy plains of
west Texas, had a particular edge to them; which is to say you
could get killed in there. In the more sophisticated big cities
the moneyed had their sedate restaurants and nightclubs and
dance floors for wining and dining, with linen tablecloths and
candlelight, music provided by waltz kings and jazz quintets
and full-blown dance orchestras. But cowboys and farmers and
lumbermen had their needs, too. Out there in a harder America, they would open the doors of a barn or a Quonset hut or a
roller-skating rink out on the edge of town on a weekend night,
hire a country band, toss some sawdust on the dance floor,
crank up the fiddles and the steel guitars, announce that the
bar was open, and you had a bubbling volcano. (Indeed, one
day when Hank was assembling another edition of the Drifting
Cowboys he escorted the boys to a pawn shop in Montgomery
and bought each of them a billy club, a leather blackjack filled
with lead. "You'll need these if you're gonna work with me," he
said.) "In some of those places," said Don Helms, the most famous of Hank's steel guitarists over the years, "they wouldn't
let you in until you showed 'em your switchblade and could
prove you'd already thrown up once. When you paid and got

in, you'd pick a table, slap your bottle on it, and throw your blade in the floor. That thing was still vibrating when they brought you a bucket of ice and some glasses." Choose your weapon: a knife, a pistol hidden in your boot, a broken beer bottle, a guitar, a chair. In the livelier houses, a chicken-wire fence was strung up to separate the band from the drinkers, and management either hired its own bouncers or had the sheriff's department on call. Some old boy would stand on a chair and shout, "By god, I wanna hear 'Tumbling Tumbleweed,'" and the wise musician broke into "Tumbling Tumbleweed" if he knew what was good for him. A country singer learned to accommodate the crowd, to sing and play loud enough to be heard over the noise of the revelers in those days before amplifiers, and how to make a fast exit when things got out of hand. The money was so good that you had little choice.

Hank's introduction to this underworld came early on, in his late teens, right there in his childhood hometown of Georgiana. Out on U.S. Highway 31, the rippled asphalt road connecting Montgomery and Mobile, there was a place called Thigpen's Log Cabin, built and operated by Fred Thigpen, a distant cousin of Hank's, who also owned the local Ford dealership. There was a dining room in the front, opening onto a walled-in skating pavilion converted to a dance hall for weekends. With cars lining the shoulder of the highway for a mile each way of Thigpen's and the adjoining Pineview Tourist Court, a collection of doll-house cabins handy for trysting, they were ready for business when the sun went down. Hank's popularity had grown steadily during that time, the early forties, when he had his regular show on WSFA and he held forth as Thigpen's major act, working three shows a night, every other weekend, for two solid years. Whenever Lillie came along, she stood beside Fred Thigpen at the front door—a formidable pair, Fred standing six-three and weighing 240 pounds—and insisted that they drive back home after the show to save money. When she didn't come, Hank would show up in the afternoon, tear into a steak grilled for him by a black cook remembered only as Eddie, wash it down with some whiskey, do the shows, and spend the night with relatives still living nearby in Avant, Chapman, and Bolling. The patrons danced while the band was playing, but they tended to crowd around the stage and listen raptly when Hank began singing in his loud, clear voice. There was the inevitable trouble, to be sure, once forcing him to break his favored Gibson guitar with the lacquered sunburst finish over the head of a drunk, but he was learning. To be sure, the lessons were coming the hard way—dealing with boisterous crowds, alternating the music between danceable tunes and roadhouse weepers, dressing for success, dealing with management—and along the way he found that a curious relationship was developing between him and his fans. The women loved the way he swayed seductively when he sang (long before Elvis Presley), and that was precisely what pissed off the young bucks, convinced he had come to steal their women; but on the other hand there was a sniff of danger emanating from this cocky scarecrow with jug ears and a sardonic smile that caused crowds to part at his coming. Hank's experiences at Thigpen's Log Cabin, when he was still a teenager, taught him everything he would need to know for the long, dark journey that lay ahead.

No sooner had the Depression abated, in the late thirties, than now there was something else to worry about. Another war was coming, the only question being when, and it had put the nation on edge. Uncertainty ruled. Do you get married and start your family and open a new business now, or do you wait to see what's going to happen? Hank Williams didn't find any of this in the comic books, his primary source of "news," but there was no escaping it. For someone just beginning to show great progress in his chosen career, this was rotten timing. He had the steady radio show every weekday on WSFA and the usual appearances out in the countryside, where his name had become well known, and he was something of a star at Thigpen's Log Cabin. He had a pretty good thing going, for a kid that age, but he got sidetracked in December of '41 when the Japanese bombed Pearl Harbor.

Hank's eyesight had corrected itself, but his back condition had steadily worsened over the years—hastened by an impromptu visit to a rodeo in Texas, playing out a childhood fantasy, where he was promptly thrown by a bull—getting him a 4-F deferment from the military draft. The Second World War was engaged now, but he wasn't a part of it. One by one the members of his band were being drafted or volunteering, and he was at home with his mother, trying to carry on alone, but it wasn't the same. (Lillie, in fact, had moved her boardinghouse to another address in Montgomery, and chosen a husband from among her boarders. His father had finally left the VA hospital system, moved back home to McWilliams, and remarried. And his sister, Irene, had taken a job at nearby Gunter Field.) The Drifting Cowboys who hadn't gone into the military were being scared off by Hank's increasing drinking. One of those was a steel guitarist, Boots Harris, who quit in disgust while they were backing up the cowboy actor turned Opry singer Tex Ritter on a tour: "We'd hear records on the

jukebox, and Hank'd say, 'Someday I'm gonna be doin' that.'
But I didn't see it coming any time soon, the way he was going.
He was pretty bad into the drink then. I said, 'If you keep
drinkin', ain't nobody in the business gonna pay us no attention.'" Later, when his hero Roy Acuff came to Montgomery
for a concert, Hank dropped in backstage to visit, but he was
drunk and received not comfort but a lecture: "You've got a
million-dollar voice, son, but a ten-cent brain." Finally, in August of '42, the booze caught up with him. He was fired at
WSFA for "habitual drunkenness."

There had never been any grand design in his career-
planning, but now it was falling apart. Oh, he had written and
recorded a song entitled "I'm Not Coming Home Anymore" in
April of that year, a dark elegy backed by a steel guitar and a
thumping bass, the first glimpse of the mournful classics still
five years away, but nothing came of it; and he had recorded a
bogus "Hank Williams Show"—a song and a few words of self-
promotion from a make-believe Fort Deposit radio station, intended as a sample to pitch himself to prospective employers.
The gig at Thigpen's Log Cabin dried up, as did all of his radio
work, and Hank was cut adrift for several months, the darkest
period of his life. In the fall of '42 he answered an ad placed by
Kaiser Shipbuilding—which offered a one-way train ticket to
Portland, Oregon, free rent, and a salary while he was being
trained in the company's shipyards—but he was drunk when
he boarded the train, then rode all the way across the country,
showed up for only one day of training and drank up his wages,
and about three weeks later wired Lillie for money so he could
get back home to Alabama. A month later he showed up in Mobile, ostensibly to take a job with the Alabama Dry Dock and

Shipbuilding Company, living with relatives down there. That didn't last long, either. The sight of a scrawny Hank Williams trying to rivet steel plates together in the service of Uncle Sam was entertainment in itself. This boy was made for picking and singing, and he knew that better than anybody.

Miss Audrey

Late in the summer of 1943, Hank found himself serving as the star attraction of a tattered medicine show on the fringes of a south Alabama community called Banks. He was being housed in a trailer, whence he would emerge hourly, like a dancing bear or a trained seal, to perform on a flatbed trailer, descending into whatever crowd might have gathered to hear his personal pitches for a "medicine" that was little more than quasi-legal alcohol, ducking back inside for a rest and some booze of his own, then running through the same routine for a fresh batch of suckers. It couldn't get much worse than this. Drinking had cost him his regular radio gig; he was a school dropout; nearly everybody he knew had gone off to war; his mother was on his case; and the wartime economy had narrowed the job opportunities. He was only a step removed from absolute rock bottom, in fact, perilously close to working the streets for loose change just as he and Tee-Tot had done during his childhood years. There had been all of that promise—as "the Singing Kid," star of his own show on WSFA, leader of his own band, a wunderkind bursting with grandiose plans—but now he had reached the pits. It was remindful of the joke about the circus roustabout who was asked if he hadn't had enough of shoveling up after elephants: "What? And give up show business?" On the cusp of his twentieth birthday, Hank seemed to have a great future behind him.

In the middle of one of those sweltering afternoons, a big four-door Oldsmobile slowed down and then stopped at the sight. The car held Audrey Mae Sheppard, an attractive twenty-year-old blonde who lived on a nearby farm with her parents and her two-year-old daughter, and her aunt Ethel; Audrey and Ethel were headed for a country music show that night in Troy, the big town in those parts. Since neither had ever seen such a sight—*a real medicine show!*—they decided to check it out, if only from the safety of Audrey's car. Through the windows they saw this skinny hillbilly in boots and a cowboy hat singing his songs and taking his bows before moving into the scattered crowd, and they were ready to fire up the engine and move on, when suddenly he was upon them, blocking their way. "Ma'am," he said, coming face-to-face with the young woman at the wheel, "don't you need some of these herbs?" But then he took a closer look, his piercing brown eyes checking out this fine specimen. "No, ma'am," he said, "I don't think you do." She was so taken aback by his audacity, and wary, that it was her aunt who issued the invitation for him to ride along with them to the club in Troy.

Hank and Audrey got their eyes and ears full of each other that night during what would become their first "date." He certainly knew which end was up on a woman, although most of his romantic explorations had come from groping with hot-blooded young girls—"snuff queens," they would later be called in country music circles—in the weeds or in the back-seats of automobiles or in that very same medicine-show trailer. But Hank had barely had a speaking relationship with any women other than his mother and his sister and his cousins, and now here was this live temptress daring him to show her something. That night Hank learned that Audrey was the oldest of three daughters of a hard-drinking cotton and peanut farmer, separated from the teenaged father of her baby daughter, and now was a high school dropout clerking at a drugstore in the little town of Brundidge. He could see that she was quite a package: smart-mouthed, feisty, slightly older than he, with handsome Creek cheekbones and a figure so striking, their own son would say decades later, that it could "melt the wax off a Dixie Cup at fifty feet."

What Hank didn't realize was that this wasn't exactly the enabler he craved, an acquiescent partner content to stand by her man through hell and high water, but rather a strident control freak. He would make that discovery soon enough, at noon the very next day, when Audrey showed up at the trailer and found him reeking of alcohol, unshaven, shirtless, drinking some hair-of-the-dog to get his day jump-started. She went to work—raising hell about his drinking, making him shave and shower, getting him dressed properly—before they got into her car for a drive. Aimlessly riding around, feeling each other out, they began swapping life stories. He admitted to her that he had been fired from WSFA for his drinking. She told him that she was a singer herself, and wasn't it a coincidence that they were both interested in show business? Maybe they could become a team, make music together. The physical attraction was pulling them toward each other like steel to a magnet. Audrey hung around for that afternoon's performances, and before the night was over he was asking her to marry him.

If he had asked more questions, he would have found out that this girl, Audrey, was a headstrong force of nature with a mind of her own, a virtual clone of the mother who had bedeviled him for most of his life. Growing up in a house full of women whose titular head was a man often weakened by drink, she had learned early on to take charge; the sort of little girl who insisted on laying the ground rules even when the game was only playing "dress-up" or orchestrating a doll wedding. She had been ignoring her daddy's rules and forging ahead on her own for a long time—driving a car when she was twelve, running off to marry a neighborhood boy when she was seventeen, mothering a child at eighteen—and it had always worked in her favor. "I knew what I wanted and I went after it," she would say years later. She could see that this boy had promise (there was his insouciant country manner and, my, how he could sing!) and with a little guidance . . . well, they could really go places together. She could see it now, their names in lights: *Tonight, Hank and Audrey Williams!* "And that," Audrey said portentously in her autobiography, "is how it started."

She wasn't quite ready to say yes to Hank's insistent marriage proposals, her first order of business being to ditch her serviceman husband, but she was tentatively signing on for the roller-coaster ride that Hank's life had already become. Escaping the medicine show, moving back into his old room in his mother's boardinghouse, alone and not yet ready to introduce Lillie and Audrey, Hank went his slipshod way. He managed to get into the Montgomery city auditorium before a big Labor Day country-and-gospel show, and when somebody noticed him drinking and lollygagging around backstage it was suggested that he go out and introduce the emcee, a performer named Hardrock Gunter. Hank grabbed Hardrock's guitar, hit the stage and began singing, got the crowd going, and the promoters had to drag him off so the show could proceed as

scheduled. Now and then he took to visiting the Sears & Roe-
buck store in Montgomery, putting down his money, wriggling
into a cramped booth with his guitar, and recording himself on
an acetate disc, coming out with an audio equivalent of a Foto-
Mat snapshot. Hank was part of the troupe accompanying the
polka band of Pee Wee King on a short tour of south Alabama,
and it was then that he sold his first song, a war ditty entitled
"(I'm Praying for the Day That) Peace Will Come," written to
order for a singer who needed a patriotic song, Hank's half of
the rights being fifty dollars cash, up front, plenty of money for
booze. There would be the inevitable rambles down to Pensacola, where he would hunker down in a room at the San Carlos Hotel, to drink and hide from both Lillie and Audrey, now
and then emerging to take the wide marble steps to the ballroom to join Pappy Neal McCormick's band. And there was
one final return to the shipyards in Mobile, where Hank and
Audrey shared a seedy hotel room for a couple of months,
working side by side with blowtorches in the innards of Liberty
ships during the day, but that would be Hank Williams's
farewell to physical labor. "This isn't it, Hank," she told him,
and he was in full agreement.

With yet another version of the Drifting Cowboys, this one
featuring the steel guitarist Don Helms, a Pappy Neal protégé
who would turn out to be his steadiest band member, Hank
soon got his career back on track by booking regular gigs in
the neighboring south Alabama towns of Andalusia and Opp.
In Andalusia, they worked the Riverside Club, one of the
biggest dance halls in the state, even busier than Thigpen's
Log Cabin, with crowds of six hundred on weekends. Hank
rented a trailer and Audrey moved in with him, Helms and the
others driving in for the shows every night from their homes in

nearby towns. Hank was being a good boy, going easy on the booze; the money was good, and Audrey was getting a monthly allotment from her husband overseas; she turned out to be an awful cook, but at least she was trying; now, if she would just ditch her husband, they could get married and live happily ever after. Joviality reigned among Hank and Don Helms and a third band member, all of them with fiancées: maybe the Cowboys would marry their cowgirls in a triple-wedding ceremony. But Hank and Audrey couldn't wait. It hadn't been easy, divorcing a soldier serving the nation overseas, and ten days after Audrey finally pulled it off early in December of '44, she said yes to Hank. They were married at a gas station in Andalusia by the owner of the place, the handiest justice of the peace they could find. Attending the service, such as it was, were a couple of pals and their girlfriends, who had to empty their pockets to help pay the justice of the peace.

The honeymoon ended in short order. Hank got royally drunk the night the Andalusia gig ended, and Audrey went ballistic. The lovebirds flew into each other, shouting and flailing away, Hank throwing all of her clothes into the mud outside the trailer and Audrey calling the cops. It was poor Don Helms's lot to go fetch Hank from the police station the next day, and when he walked in, greatly embarrassed, he saw Hank sitting morosely on a bench in his cell, staring bullets at him: "Well, what do you want me to do, stand on my head? Get me out of here." Helms paid the thirty dollars, and they headed out the door. "Come back and see us, now, Hank," one the policemen chirped sarcastically, an indication that it had been a long night for everyone concerned. "Y'all can all go to hell," Hank snapped over his shoulder as he took his leave.

·　　·　　·

There was no putting if off any longer. The time had come for Hank to introduce his bride to his mama. Leaving her daughter, Lycrecia, behind with her parents until she and Hank could get settled, Audrey got behind the wheel of her Oldsmobile for the drive to Montgomery, Hank navigating from the shotgun seat, having long ago lost his driver's license on drunk-driving escapades. Hank had barely been introduced to the boarder Lillie had married, a husky Cajun-bred Army Air Corps sergeant named J. C. Bozard, but it was about to become a moot point the way Lillie and the sergeant were slugging it out. Lon Williams, on the other hand, had found peace with a placid second wife back home in McWilliams after his final release from VA hospitals and fathered a little girl who was walking by now. Parking at the curb in front of 236 Catoma Street, Lillie's latest boardinghouse, Mr. and Mrs. Hank Williams walked onto the front porch, with not a little trepidation, to announce that they were home.

In fairy tales, in the best of all worlds, a man's mother graciously steps aside when he brings home the girl he has chosen, after all, to take her place. *Welcome to the family, dear,* is what he will hear from his mother if he's lucky. The bride's proper response is *May I call you Mom?* But this was no fairy tale. Sparks arced between Audrey and Lillie from the first instant they made eye contact. "She's probably going to ask, 'Where'd you find this whore?'" Audrey had said to Hank, and that's more or less the way it went. There was this to be said for Lillie: for twenty years, throughout the Depression and into the early years of the war, and without any help from a stable husband and father, she had thrown herself into the earnest support of a talented but troublesome son who often resented the way she went about it. There was this to be said for Audrey, however new she was to the scene: she knew talent when she saw it, and if she could straighten this boy out, truly become his helpmate, it would get him off the medicine-show and honky-tonk circuit and sure as hell spring her from the drugstore in Brundidge. Both women loved Hank, in their respective ways, but the only way this arrangement would benefit him was if they teamed up and worked together. That turned out to be too much to ask of either of them. They were so alike in personality—needy, domineering, unforgiving of Hank's weaknesses, desperate to share his successes—that they spent their efforts fighting over him like dogs shredding a rag doll. So Hank and Audrey moved into the boardinghouse as man and wife, and thus was engaged a tempestuous threesome that would give pause to several generations of curbside psychologists.

The one thing the two women could agree upon was that something had to be done about Hank's drinking. By now, ironically, as he neared the official drinking age, he could be clinically classified as an alcoholic. It had begun innocently enough—it always does—with those first sips of filched moonshine as a twelve-year-old outside the lumber-camp dance halls in the deep woods. It continued when he shared nips of Tee-Tot's exotic mixture of whiskey and tea on the streets of Georgiana and Greenville. Alcohol was everywhere, cheap and available in spite of Prohibition laws, and he could argue that it gave him temporary relief from his back pains and the incessant demands of his domineering mother and now his wife. He was willing to forget the downsides of hangovers and general fuckups—as alcoholics always do—in exchange for the good times. His dance with liquor had intensified when he entered the adult world of honky-tonks, where booze was the oil that put everything into motion, making that the last place someone who can't do without the stuff should be. Hank was capable of going months at a time without giving whiskey a thought; but something was always coming up to send him into a spin—a fight with Lillie or Audrey, a nasty crowd, unseen demons—and that's all it took. He simply couldn't "hold his likker," as the boys put it, and once he opened a bottle there was nothing to do but drain it dry. He was unsupervised, working for himself instead of a boss who might check his breath at the door, and the condition thus was overlooked: *Just be there on time and give us a good show.* When he got away with it, everything was fine. When it didn't, there was hell to pay.

Whiskey, everyone agreed, was the curse of the working class. In the middle of the Depression, in Akron, Ohio, a surgeon and a broker had come up with the idea of a self-help group called Alcoholics Anonymous, an approach, at once simple and sophisticated, to break the cycle of drinking. Alcoholism was being called a disease by then, something that could be brought under control if the "afflicted" understood there was a problem and was willing to correct it by gathering regularly with other alcoholics at AA meetings to share experiences. Try telling that to an Alabama country boy who's been told all his life that drinking is a sin, a moral weakness. (Drunk: "Help me out, Doc. Drinking's cost me my wife, my kids, my house, my car, my job, and my health." Doctor: "Have you ever thought about AA?" Drunk: "Aw, hell, it ain't *that* bad.") In the Bible Belt South of Hank Williams's time, a propensity for drink was not something to be handled with hope and forgiveness; it was, rather, the Lord's business in the eternal struggle with Satan, and that's exactly what he got from the two women in his life. When he was sober Audrey and

Lillie were fully behind him, but when he got drunk they came down on him like buzzards. So he went underground—as alcoholics always do—trying sobriety as long as he could stand it, until he snapped and went off on another binge. He drank to celebrate his joys, and he drank to forget his sorrows. It was a cycle he never learned to break.

Early in 1945, with the entertainment business beginning to pick up as the war neared its end, Hank returned to WSFA with a live show every day from the studio at the Jefferson Davis Hotel. This was the anchor he needed, both a place to call home and a showcase for his talents, and he took full measure of the opportunity no matter what was going on at the big house between Lillie and Audrey. Always quick to learn, a "fast read," Hank had become a slick radio host with an inviting demeanor—a guy whose natural pronunciation of "picture" was "pitcher" and who didn't have to practice his *y'alls* and *ain'ts*—and the show became so popular that the hostess of an afternoon talk show bitched to WSFA about his flood of sponsors, and so many fans began crowding the lobby of the Jeff Davis in hopes of seeing Hank and the Cowboys that the hotel's management insisted he and the boys use a backdoor entrance when they came to work. All good things flowed from that radio show: fan mail began piling up, sponsors clamored to buy time, honky-tonks and civic groups all over the listening area started upping the price for personal appearances, and word of this new talent began to spread among such stars of the Grand Ole Opry as Ernest Tubb when they happened to be in town to play concerts at the auditorium. Hank had clearly become the biggest name in country music in south Alabama, and when he insisted that WSFA give him an exclusive deal—no other country acts on the station—he got no argument from management.

He was writing songs now, too, and when there were enough of them he paid a local printer to publish a collection in pamphlet form, *Songs of Hank Williams, "The Drifting Cowboy."* The price was thirty-five cents for "handling" ("You send the money and I'll handle it"). When that edition sold out within a year, he followed it with another, this one a more effusive issue containing thirty songs and three photos: *Hank Williams and His Drifting Cowboys, Stars of WSFA, Deluxe Song Book.* In the grand tradition of touring musicians, the songbooks were pitched over the radio and hawked at the door before and after road shows. There wasn't a keeper in the bunch, at least none of the tunes that would remain as his legacy, but there were some hints of the mournful autobiographical dirges to come. There was the rough draft of "Honky Tonkin'," one of Hank's signature songs, and three angry love-gone-wrong ditties that surely gave Audrey pause as she stood at the front door of auditoriums and clubs selling the songbooks: "I Don't Care (If Tomorrow Never Comes)" and "My Love for You (Has Turned to Hate)" and "Never Again (Will I Knock on Your Door)." Tossed in for good measure was a smattering of moralistic gospel musings like "Wealth Won't Save Your Soul," not that Hank was a Bible-toting proselytizer but because Jesus was good for business. The songbooks contained the lyrics, not the music, for the simple reason that Hank couldn't read music and he wasn't about to pay somebody to translate it for him.

Life out there on the road was more profitable than ever, with Hank's rising popularity, but more violent for the same reason. Flush with success, he had gained a strutting confidence that came across to many as cockiness. Often, as the

troupe was riding back home after playing a juke joint in south
Alabama, Hank rode in the backseat holding a towel of ice to
his bruises; once, a drunk had bitten a chunk of meat from
around his eyebrow; more than once, he and the band were
forced to fight their way to safety by brandishing guitars and
whiskey bottles and even the screw-off legs of the steel guitar.
"Hank never *started* any trouble," said Don Helms, "but it
sure came to him. It was always the guys. They were jealous of
him for the money they figured he was making, and they resented the way the women swooned over him. Hank didn't win
many fights, but he sure as hell didn't back down." (A hulking
professional wrestler named Cannonball Nichols took a brief
fling as a Drifting Cowboy, not for his proficiency on the bass
fiddle but because he knew a mean half nelson.) Hank had
shifted into full songwriting mode by now, buoyed by the success of his songbooks, and he found inspiration everywhere.
The Cowboys always knew they were nearing home when they
caught sight of the searchlight sweeping above the Montgomery airport; "Wake up, Hank, I saw the light," somebody
said from the backseat on one of those late-night returns, and
he knew he had the title for a song, albeit a gospel: "I Saw the
Light."

Home wasn't necessarily a place where Hank could kick back
and lick his wounds before heading out again. Audrey—"Miss
Ordrey," in his twang—had begun wresting control from Lillie
almost immediately, taking over booking dates and paying the
band and generally orchestrating Hank's life. Worst of all, she
bought herself a fringed cowgirl outfit and insisted on singing
with the band in a voice so shrill and indescribably bad—like
the off-key soprano in a church choir who always manages to

screech above the rest—that Hank resorted to turning off her microphone without telling her. ("It's bad enough to have a wife who wants to sing," he said, "but it's hell to have one who wants to sing but can't.") Now, when he got home, Hank had both of the women in his life on his case, almost always about his drinking, and sometimes things turned violent. Lillie's boardinghouse had the makings of a television sitcom with its varied characters, a mélange of squabbling couples and ambitious young secretaries and rural politicians and, of course, its full-time residents. Fearing for his physical safety, J. C. Bozard literally fled his brief marriage to Lillie, who was soon romancing yet another boarder. A couple named Bernice and Doyle Turner joined the band and moved into the house when Don Helms was drafted toward the end of the war; but Doyle was an alcoholic, like Hank, leading to violent fights with his wife that once ended in gunfire. Now and then Hank would snap, lying up drunk in his room when he found himself unable to write, finally hauling ass to the San Carlos Hotel in Pensacola. On such occasions, Audrey would slink home to her parents' farm near Banks, threatening never to return. Teeming with animosities, Lillie's place resembled a war zone.

Hank's growing celebrity worked both ways, of course. More than once he showed up drunk and unable to perform, or didn't show up at all, causing all sorts of consternation among promoters left holding the bag in the small towns and communities south of Montgomery. Often WSFA was forced to air canned reruns of his radio broadcasts when he called in "sick." Early in 1945 he was delivered to a sanitarium in Prattville to be treated for alcoholism, which in those days, in Alabama, usually meant being dried out and bed-rested for three or four days. He was still popping in backstage at the municipal auditorium, sometimes drunk and unmanageable, whenever troupes came to town. Established stars like Tubb would report back to Nashville that they really ought to take a listen to this kid, that he had the stuff the Opry was looking for, but the word was already spreading: *Williams, Hank. Unreliable.* In that small world of south Alabama, Hank had gotten so big that WSFA couldn't fire him in spite of his transgressions. But in a larger world, where there was more at stake, most especially the carefully preened reputation of the Grand Ole Opry as a wholesome "family" institution, managers quite frankly didn't want to mess with him.

A measure of calm came to the Williams household in late '46 when Hank put together enough money to rent a house a few blocks away from his mother's boardinghouse. It was the first time he had ever lived under what he might call his own roof. Audrey went to her parents' farm and fetched her daughter, Lycrecia, now turning five years old, and the three of them settled in for what they hoped would be a normal family life. Peace settled over Hank like a warm blanket. He treated the little girl as though she were his own blood kin. The marriage wasn't exactly the way a WSFA program director described it in Hank's second songbook—"He is happily married and he and 'Miss Audrey' are already famous as a team"—but it was as close as he had ever been to domestic tranquillity.

Fred Rose

All news was local in the rural South of those days. You might have become a hotshot in New York or Paris or even Shanghai, bubba, but you'd better not have forgotten your raising. In the summer of 1932, a gifted athlete named Percy Beard had left his home in Pine Apple, Alabama, about thirty miles from where young Hiram Williams was living with his mother and his sister in Georgiana, and taken a train all the way across the country to compete in the Olympics in Los Angeles. Those games preceded the famous '36 Olympics in Berlin, where the great African American runner Jesse Owens would literally trample on Adolf Hitler's ideas of an Aryan master race right there in his own backyard. At any rate, Beard ran alongside Owens in '32, bringing back medals of his own, and for days he sat at home savoring his triumphs, waiting for someone in Pine Apple to at least ask him where he had been and how things had gone. Weeks passed until finally he came across a brief item in the Personals column of the county's weekly newspaper: "Percy Beard, son of Mr. and Mrs. G. W. Beard of Pine Apple, recently returned from California, where he participated in a footrace."

This provincial thinking was all too familiar to Hank. His wife and his mother certainly wanted to see him reach for the stars—indeed, pushed him relentlessly—but Hank and many other poor southern country boys of his generation felt a reluctance to "rise above your raisin'," as they were repeatedly cautioned by their peers. A certain xenophobia was loose on the land, a fear of strangers and the dark unknown beyond the borders of one's home country, and there was no doubt that this had its roots in the Civil War. The South was the only region in the nation that had suffered the degradations of defeat and occupation by a "foreign" army. That war was about slavery, not states' rights or some other noble purpose, but never mind: the psychic fallout from the South's loss was overwhelming in places like rural Alabama. Southerners born half a century after the war's end, as was Hank, were still burdened with a sense that they were inferior to other Americans. The statistics were there, showing that the South might never recover from its foolhardiness, and people in the rest of the country made sure they never forgot. Rural southerners were constantly reminded that they were redneck "hillbillies" who dipped snuff, made their own whiskey, married their cousins, and talked funny. Consequently, they turned inward, gave the world twenty-four hours to get out of town, and stayed home. Given their lack of self-confidence, this was the easy way for them to go.

There were times when it seemed that Hank might be content to enjoy being the big frog in a little pond, just stick with what he had and forget about rolling the dice, even though it was clear that he had outgrown south Alabama. He had completed his basic training in the hairy world of honky-tonks and schoolhouses and medicine shows and low-watt radio stations—had paid his dues—and now it was time, as his fishing buddies were wont to say, to "fish or cut bait." There he sat in sleepy Montgomery, an accomplished performer holding a growing portfolio of songs he had written, simply running in place, taking the easy way out. With no music publishers or recording

studios in town, he had been forced to pay a printer to produce
his songbooks and to run by the Sears store to make crude van-
ity recordings of some of his songs. Meanwhile, elsewhere, ex-
citing possibilities were opening up. The commercial period in
country music had begun on a day in 1927, in Bristol on the
Tennessee-Virginia line, when a recording engineer-cum-
talent scout named Ralph Peer uncrated his bulky equipment
and announced he was holding auditions for local performers.
He had a very good day at the office. When he packed up and
left, he had signed the first commercial stars in what would be
called "hillbilly" music: a group from the Clinch Mountains
known as the Carter Family; and a tubercular Mississippi yodeler named Jimmie Rodgers, who had been driving a cab in
Asheville, North Carolina.

Two years earlier, in 1925, the 50,000-watt radio giant
WSM in Nashville had introduced a Saturday night barn dance
called the Grand Ole Opry, four hours of live music attracting
scores of front-porch fiddlers and nasally warblers and other
raw talents who were being flushed out of the distant crannies
of the southern outback by men such as Peer. What had begun
as a means of selling life insurance for the National Life & Accident Insurance Company (WSM stood for "We Shield Millions") was turning into a wildly popular venture that was
making Nashville a veritable hillbilly heaven. If you wanted to
make it in country music, you got yourself to Nashville, where
the foundation was being laid for what would later become Music City U.S.A., locus of all the nation's country music publishers, recording studios, side musicians, managers, and
agents. Now and then a singer based elsewhere might make it
("Aw, hell, it don't matter where you cut [your record] at,"
Merle Haggard of California would say decades later, "it's what

you put in the groove"), but in the postwar forties the rainbow began in Nashville.

Hank had made a halfhearted run on Nashville toward the end of the Second World War, the only result being that he got his feelings hurt. He had taken a train up, found WSM, and, unannounced, asked to speak to one of the Opry announcers whose voice he had heard wavering in and out on his radio in Montgomery. "There was this guy with blue jeans and a white hat," remembered Judd Collins. "He said, 'I'm Hank Williams. Charlie Holt from WSFA told me to come up here and see you. He said you'd tell me what I have to do to get on the Opry.'" Hank was told there were no shortcuts, that he would have to audition for the Opry's general manager, Jack Stapp. "He wouldn't go see Stapp. He said, 'You tell [him] I'm here.' I think he was disappointed that I couldn't take him by the hand and say, 'Hank, you're on the Opry tonight at eight.'" Hank had been on the right track toward the Opry, but he didn't know how to capitalize on it. The system worked a lot like professional baseball, where a player steadily worked his way up step by step, from Class D on up to Triple-A, until he proved he was ready for the top rung, the major leagues. In country music, you worked the boondocks and little radio stations (Class D) moving up to progressively larger markets until you were deemed ready. Hank got back on the train and rode home to Montgomery that day, tail between his legs, and endured another year of working at WSFA and playing the joints.

Strut around he might, back home in Alabama—picking fights, lording it over the lesser talents, letting it be known that he had personally opened shows for the likes of Tubb and Acuff—but he still lacked the genuine confidence to insinuate himself in Nashville. There had to be a better plan before he made another attempt at cracking the big leagues, and this time the one true talent of "Miss Ordrey" came into play. *Go through the back door as a songwriter,* Audrey proposed, *and there's where you start.* The one music publisher in Nashville at that time was Acuff-Rose, housed near downtown on Franklin Road, seeded in '42 with Roy Acuff's money. The "Rose"? That would be Fred Rose, a pianist and songwriter and music doctor who knew talent when he heard it. At daybreak on September 14, 1946, a Saturday, Hank and Audrey boarded a train in Montgomery and headed for Nashville.

Hank couldn't have ordered up a more sympathetic ear. Slender and balding, with failing eyesight, Fred Rose was forty-nine years old on the day of their first meeting (Hank would turn twenty-three the next week) and, like Hank, had grown up virtually fatherless, on the Ohio River in southern Indiana. He had taught himself to play the piano at the age of seven, run away from home, and in his teens was making a living as a musician in Chicago during the jazz age. An accomplished pianist and a glib songwriter, he put together quite a portfolio for himself during the twenties and thirties. He was a featured performer for a while on radio WBBM in Chicago; had a show called "Freddie Rose's Song Shop," wherein listeners proposed a song title and he composed an original tune on the spot; was half of a twin-piano feature on the network radio show of big-band leader Paul Whiteman; toured the Midwest with a trio called the Vagabonds; and worked the speakeasies whenever times got bad. He was the prototypical Tin Pan Alley songwriter, able to conjure a song about anything, for anybody, at the drop of a hat. He wrote "Red Hot Mama" for Sophie

Tucker, had hits of his own with "'Deed I Do" and "Honest and Truly," and even went to California (on a thirty-five-dollar-a-week salary in the Depression) to write songs to order for the cowboy star Gene Autry.

Rose had known his troubles, too. His drinking had turned into full-blown alcoholism during the Chicago days, getting him fired from WBBM and pushing him along to New York City, where he dabbled at doctoring tunes for musicals being prepared for Broadway, but shortly plummeted to playing the piano at strip joints and sleeping at night in the men's restrooms with thoughts of suicide. Two divorces and all of that traveling had stripped him of his two sons and what money he had earned. He managed to get the alcoholism under control after becoming a born-again Christian Scientist, and finally found a home when he literally took a wrong turn during a rainstorm on a tour with his trio and wound up in Nashville. That was in 1942. The white-collar burghers were calling Nashville the "Athens of the South," showing tourists their elegant Victorian mansions and Vanderbilt University and the city's re-creation of the Parthenon, and they didn't want to acknowledge the presence of all these hillbillies drifting into town for the Opry. Fred Rose was immediately hired as a pianist by WSM, which had built one of the premier radio orchestras in the nation. He didn't know or care much at all about country music, but that changed when he saw Roy Acuff cry what Rose perceived to be genuine tears when he sang "Wabash Cannonball" and his sacred songs on the stage of the Opry. Acuff hired him to cowrite and produce songs of his own in sheet form, and soon they were creating Acuff-Rose, the first music-publishing venture in town. Fred married a third and last time, bought a modest brick house, and became a sort of guru to the writers and performers arriving in Nashville almost daily.

The legend surrounding that first meeting between Hank and Fred Rose makes a lot better story than what really happened. In the fantasy, according to self-serving accounts by Lillie Williams and Wesley Rose, the long-estranged son who had by now joined Fred as the accountant at Acuff-Rose, Hank and Audrey stumble into Fred's office, unannounced, to find Fred and Wesley playing Ping-Pong on their lunch break. This pushy, attractive blonde asks if they will listen to "some songs my husband has written." Hank sings a half dozen tunes and the Roses are impressed, but Fred, wanting to make sure Hank is really that good—that indeed he has written the songs himself—proposes a test: go into that room over there and write a song about a girl who ditches her poor-boy lover and chooses to marry for money instead. Hank comes out thirty minutes later with "Mansion on the Hill," signs a songwriting contract, and is on his way to greatness. Not true, by a mile.

In fact, Hank was there by Rose's invitation. Among the more promising performers in the Acuff-Rose stable was a Kentucky singer whose stage name was Molly O'Day, in search of new material for herself, who remembered a show in Montgomery when a local boy named Hank Williams got multiple encores for his emotional reworking of an old country standard entitled "Tramp on the Street." Hank had tinkered with the original version, even published it in one of his WSFA songbooks under "Author Unknown," and at Molly O'Day's request gave her a copy of the lyrics. Word finally reached Fred Rose, who had been trying to find fresh material for O'Day, and he began to correspond with Hank. Fred's interest was further stimulated when Hank sent him acetates of several songs he had written. He invited Hank to Nashville on that Saturday in September of '46 for an audition.

Fred needed original songs, not another singer, but when he met Hank and Audrey at the Nashville railroad station that day he was struck by what he saw: a swaggering hillbilly in jeans and a cowboy hat stepping off the train, guitar case in hand, with a panache that implied he must be somebody. The three of them went straight to the offices of WSM in the National Life & Accident Insurance Company building and set to work. Hank strummed his guitar and sang a half dozen of his songs, and before the day was over he had signed a standard contract with Acuff-Rose as a songwriter, but not as a performer. (There's no evidence either way, but it's hard to imagine that Hank and Audrey wouldn't have finagled tickets to see the Opry that night, their first glimpse of the stage he would make famous within three years.) A couple of weeks later, in his primitive handwriting and on Audrey's personalized stationery, Hank scrawled a note to Rose: "Here is the two songs you asked for, and the recordings of them. If you can use more at any time, let me know and what types." Rose countered with a comment that would dog their collaborations forever, raising the lingering question of just who had written what in Hank's songs: "I must change the lyrics around in order to make them consistent. These will be minor changes, and will not interfere with what you have already written." In the ensuing months, Molly O'Day would record four of those tunes.

Clearly, Fred Rose had seen in Hank Williams more than just a songwriter willing to work cheap. He had heard the warnings about Hank's drinking from his partner, Acuff, and just about

everybody else he asked, but he had also heard that voice—as
stark and direct and pained as a van Gogh painting—and he
couldn't forget it. By the middle of December, only three
months after their first meeting, Fred had Hank in a studio to
make his first recordings. The Sterling label out of New York
City had called, wanting to jump on the "hillbilly" bandwagon,
and Fred said he had found just the right guy. Hank had gotten
on a bus alone this time, leaving Audrey at home to stew, and
showed up in Nashville two days ahead of time so he would be
rested. Thinking the current Drifting Cowboys were just a
bunch of amateurs, not quite ready for prime time, Fred had
hired the veteran Willis Brothers and a fourth man; they would
be called the Oklahoma Wranglers for this session. One of the
boys, Vic Willis, wasn't particularly impressed by Hank when
they met for rehearsals the morning of the session: "None of us
saw any potential in him. He was dirty, wore this beat-up cowboy hat, and looked a lot older than twenty-three. He was so
thin and pathetic looking, he could sit down and cross his legs
and both feet would be flat on the floor." But let it be noted that
when they all went to lunch and a waitress asked if they
wanted a beer, Hank declined, saying, "You don't know ol'
Hank. Hank don't just have *one* beer." Clear-eyed and sober,
ready to go to work, Hank signed his name to a contract Fred
handed him, agreeing to work for union scale and waiving his
right to future royalties.

They set up in WSM's Castle Studio ("Castle of the Air," the
station called itself), in the downtown Tulane Hotel, to cut four
songs in three hours, all of them Hank's compositions: "Wealth
Won't Save Your Soul," "Calling You," "When God Comes and
Gathers His Jewels," and "Never Again," the latter the only
secular tune. The relatively sophisticated Willis Brothers

winced at some of Hank's backcountry pronunciations—
"wealth won't save your *purr* wicked soul"—but Rose over-
ruled them when, try as he might, he couldn't get Hank to say
"poor" properly. When it was over, Hank took his check for
$250 and had it cashed at the hotel before boarding the bus for
Montgomery. The four backup musicians cashed their $500
check, and Vic Willis was still shaking his head: "For a man
like that to make that kind of impression on mankind, he had to
be a genius. Education might've ruined him."

Hank Williams's first record was released the next month,
in January of 1947—"Calling You" on one side, "Never
Again" on the other—and if matters had been left to Sterling
Records it would have died a stillbirth. They didn't know how
to cut records or press them; but, worse, they didn't know what
they had on their hands. In their own catalog, in fact, they gave
high marks to the Oklahoma Wranglers but dismissed Hank as
an "Acuff-type of hillbilly." *Billboard* magazine, the bible of
the music industry, thought differently—"With real spiritual
qualities in his pipes, singing with the spirit of a camp meeting, Hank Williams makes his bow an auspicious one"—and
that review, with enlightened promotion by Acuff-Rose, en-
sured decent sales. Rose hated the pejorative "hillbilly" label
(indeed, he had recently run an ad in *Billboard* declaiming it),
and he knew how to promote Acuff-Rose's products at the
source: mailing records and sheet music to country radio stations, following up with personal visits from the company's in-
house promoter.

Obviously, Fred felt he was on to something. Three months
after that first session, in February of '47, Hank was back in
the same studio for another. By now Rose had thoroughly
combed through Hank's songbooks and "demo" tapes, and this

time he had picked four secular songs—among them "Honky Tonkin'" and "Pan American"—that veered toward a vision he was beginning to develop, of Hank as a rawboned roadhouse balladeer. Hank had written "Pan American" as a tribute to one of the trains that blew through Greenville and Georgiana during his youth, the Pan American Clipper, and its melody was so close to Acuff's "Wabash Cannonball" that the writers of that one, the Carter Family, could have sued him for plagiarism. Every country singer needed a train song, though, and this would be Hank's first. The most notable aspect of "Honky Tonkin'" was that Rose, for the first time, chose to clean up Hank's references to alcohol, the bane of both men's lives: Hank's "We'll get a quart of whiskey and get up in the air" became Fred's "If you go to the city, baby, you will find me there." And there was another new wrinkle: working without drums to establish the rhythm, Fred and the WSM staff musicians he had hired to back this session came up with what they called a "crack" backbeat alternating with the bass fiddle— the pulse of the song, *boom-chuck, boom-chuck*, the basis for Johnny Cash's signature sound a generation later—by keeping time on the deadened bass strings of an electric guitar. Closer, ever closer, a new voice was coming up over the horizon. Fred Rose wasn't so much orchestrating the changes as he was allowing them to evolve.

As for Hank; well, hell, all he wanted to do was make music and have a snort of whiskey when nobody was looking. He might be able to flaunt his new status as a "Sterling recording artist"—something that thoroughly flummoxed his detractors at WSFA, who couldn't quite understand his popularity and always seemed on the verge of firing him for his indiscretions—

but to Hank it was business as usual. He was back on the road, playing schoolhouses during the week and gin joints on weekends, once even taking a regular gig playing at the stockyards in Montgomery (the promoters fired him, figuring they could save the money and the trouble he was costing them, only to rehire him when the usual crowds of 250 cattlemen fell to almost nothing the next Saturday). At a roadhouse in Fort Deposit, one of those places where a chicken-wire fence separated the band from the crowd, a drunk wearing work boots and overalls but little else bolted in from the parking lot, firing a pistol at random ("Talk about huntin' for a table," said one of the band members). On one of his sporadic toots, Hank passed out on a Montgomery street; with automobiles calmly steering around the prone body, the cops came, dragged him to safety, and took him not to jail but home to Audrey, a fate worse than the drunk tank. Hank and Audrey were still slugging it out, tensions abating only when Hank allowed her to thump the bass fiddle and sing off-key in her godawful church soprano now and then. Poor little Lycrecia was being steadily shuttled back and forth between the rental house in Montgomery and Audrey's parents' farm in Banks, depending on the level of hostilities between Hank and Audrey. The revolving members of the Drifting Cowboys loved it when Hank got his first full-blown "write-up" in a Montgomery paper, concluding with the revelation that "Mr. and Mrs. Hank Williams lead a model domestic life."

Both Hank and Fred knew that Sterling Records wasn't the answer, so Fred went shopping in New York for the right label. He knocked on doors at RCA, Columbia, Decca, and Capitol but something kept each of them from being the right fit. (Hank revealed his trust and loyalty to Fred when he got a call from the man at Decca the moment Rose walked out the door, asking, "What can Fred Rose do for you?" "He's got you calling me, ain't he?" Hank said before hanging up.) Then Rose discovered that the mammoth Loews Corporation, having seen labels like RCA make millions of dollars from selling songs from its own lavish movie musicals, had decided to start a label of its own, MGM Records (for Metro-Goldwyn-Mayer). Better yet, the man in charge at MGM was Frank Walker, a veteran who knew music inside and out, the man who had discovered the black blues singer Bessie Smith for Columbia the very year Hiram Williams was born. Best of all, Walker had spent years scouring the countryside for talent of every ilk and had a full appreciation for the roots of Hank's music. MGM was dead serious, pouring millions of dollars to convert an old munitions factory into a record-pressing plant, making distribution deals with Zenith radio stores and a network of independent distributors, promising to offer cut-rate "introductory" prices, and signing established artists like Jimmy Dorsey and Kate Smith whose contracts had run out. To that stable he was adding Hank Williams. Fred Rose would call all of the shots about what and how Hank recorded, and MGM would handle promotion and merchandising. This time, Hank's contract as an artist called for him to receive royalties.

Sensing the importance of Hank's first records on the MGM label, Fred trashed the cuts made during their first session when he deemed that the backup musicians, the Drifting Cowboys who were available, weren't up to snuff. He wanted the very best, and that turned out to be, essentially, Red Foley's Opry band. They went into the studio on a day in April of 1947 and came away with two of Hank's first real keepers: "Move It

on Over" and "I Saw the Light." The latter was classic Hank
in its inception (the title had come to him on that night, years
earlier, when somebody in the car saw the lights from the airport signaling that they were nearing Montgomery) and its
message: a misbegotten wretch finds the Lord, sees "the light,"
and vows to turn his life around. Rose withheld the release of
"Light" for a full year and a half, primarily because his partner,
Acuff, wanted to release his own version first, but also because
of what became of "Move It On Over" when it was rushed into
stores only six weeks after it was cut. Hank's good-natured and
lively tale of a wastrel husband literally being forced to spend
the night in the doghouse made the *Billboard* charts and took
off. "Move It On Over" changed everything.

Predictably, on the charts and in the chips for the first time,
Hank began to spend money exactly like somebody who'd
never had any. He made a down payment on a $10,000 house
in Montgomery. He picked out a touring-size Packard. He
bought Audrey her first fur coat. He helped buy a bigger
boardinghouse for Lillie, who had married yet another boarder,
this one an amiable cabdriver turned carpenter named W. W.
"Bill" Stone. With not a little bit of help from Audrey, the
money was flying out the door—for clothes, for cars, for furniture, for booze, for five-dollar tips on fifty-cent breakfasts—
and in spite of earning upwards of $20,000 on his songwriting
alone in 1947 he was scrambling to keep up with his mortgage
payment. Like a Roman candle, he had zoomed to his apex and
then suddenly plummeted to earth.

When Rose failed in late '47 to land a regular gig for Hank on
WLAC in Nashville, one that would have put him literally

steps away from the Opry, Hank fell apart. The four Drifting
Cowboys had bought glittery matching outfits, in anticipation
of making it to Nashville, but now they were having to pay for
the thirty-dollar suits with little regular income. They were
back on the road again, to the same low-rent venues they
thought they would never see again, sometimes with Hank and
sometimes without him. ("The last time I saw him, all I saw
was his boots," said J. C. Sims, an acquaintance from Hank's
childhood. "They were playing the schoolhouse in Starlington
and those long ol' boots were sticking out the back window of
their car. Everybody knew he was passed out drunk, but the
show went on anyway.") WSFA ran out of patience and fired
him again. Hank and the band got their last regular job in
Montgomery, at a dance hall called the 31 Club, where too often he showed up drunk and unable to perform. There was a
disaster of larger magnitude when he was booed off the stage at
a downtown theater while warming up the crowd for a couple of
Opry stars. That led to another incarceration, if that's the
word, in the sanitarium in Prattville, and, soon after, a letter
from Fred Rose:

> Wesley tells me you called this morning for more
> money, after me wiring you four hundred dollars just the
> day before yesterday. We have gone as far as we can go at
> this time and cannot send you any more. Hank, I have
> tried to be a friend of yours but you refuse to let me be
> one, and I feel that you are just using me for a good thing
> and this is where I quit. You have been very unfair, call-
> ing my house in the middle of the night and I hope that
> you will not let it happen again, as it isn't fair to Lorene.
> When you get ready to straighten out, let me know and

maybe we can pick up where we left off, but for the present I am fed up with all your foolishness.

And then, thoroughly fed up herself, Audrey filed for divorce on the grounds that her husband "has a violent and ungovernable temper. He drinks a great deal, and during the last month he has been drunk most of the time. My nervous system has been upset and I am afraid to live with him any longer."

Three years and four months had passed since their impromptu wedding at the service station in Andalusia, and many were in wonderment that the union had lasted that long. "I never doubted that they loved each other," said Don Helms, speaking for those who knew them best, "but they just had some funny ways of showing it." They cursed, drank, shouted, and threw things at each other, including punches. Hank had thought peace was at hand when he bought the house—Lycrecia would always contend that Hank was "a good daddy" who took well to the notion, at least, of being the breadwinner to a wife and daughter—but he quickly discovered that this wasn't the way to Audrey's heart. She didn't want to be a cowboy's sweetheart, somebody's faithful cook and housekeeper, a rock in a storm. She wanted to be an equal partner, precisely one-half of the show, envisioning herself as Miss Audrey, in her fringed cowgirl get-up, yodeling and harmonizing beside her husband as they rode off together into the sunset. The problem with that vision was that she simply didn't have the voice and she certainly didn't have the patience to ride out the bad times—Lord knows, Hank had given her plenty—and when she couldn't have it all *now* she bailed out and took her daughter back home to her parents' farm.

Hank sold the house, recovered his $2,200 deposit for
something to live on, and moved back into Lillie's boardinghouse, where often in that spring of '48 he was seen sprawled
on the front-porch swing in his boots, cowboy hat, and spangled suit—all dressed up with no place to go—like a shell-
shocked veteran home from the war. So lonesome he could cry,
he slept late, piddled at writing songs, tried to ignore Lillie's
glares and deprecations, guzzled whiskey, listened to the radio, devoured his comic books (*Joe Palooka* and *Ozark Ike*
were his favorites) and his romance magazines in order to escape reality, and might have found female comfort if he hadn't
gotten into the habit of passing out by sundown. His train had
left the station without him, it seemed. Once more, Fred Rose
typed a letter to his anguished protégé:

> You are destined for big things in the recording and
> songwriting field and you are the only one that can ruin
> this opportunity. In the future, forget the firewater and let
> me take care of your business and you'll be a big name in
> this business. . . . Remember that women are revengeful
> and do all in their power to wreck a man when they sepa-
> rate from him and the only way to win is for the man to
> become successful instead.

Back in the summer of '47 there had been a disappointing
recording session that produced a couple of songs Hank would
always use as metaphors for failure: "Fly Trouble," a talking-
blues number, written by Fred Rose and a blackface comedy
team known as Jamup and Honey, that was supposed to compete with the hit "Smoke! Smoke! Smoke! (That Cigarette)";
and "On the Banks of the Old Pontchartrain," a narrative

Hank based on a bad poem scribbled on a postcard he received from a fan in Louisiana. Neither was right for him, and he knew it: "I just hope it don't turn out to be another 'Fly Trouble' or 'Pontchartrain,'" he would say over the years when a new record was about to be released. On back-to-back days in November of that year, he had put down the tracks for eight more songs, in MGM's anticipation of a recording ban by the newly formed American Federation of Musicians, that would have mixed results: "Rootie Tootie" was another ill-advised selection of a clever little Rose ditty, but "A Mansion on the Hill," "Honky Tonkin'," and "I'm a Long Gone Daddy" (acknowledging a spouse who would "rather fight than eat") would make the charts and eventually join the Hank Williams *oeuvre*. While Hank was frittering away his days and waiting for the divorce papers to wend through the courts during that sultry spring in Montgomery, Fred was still on the case in Nashville in spite of his deep concerns about his boy's personal life. Just as he was orchestrating the release of some cuts from the November sessions and looking for a way to get Hank out of Montgomery, he was stunned to receive a giddy vacation postcard from Norfolk, Virginia, a month after the Williamses' divorce was to have gone through: "Having Big Time, Hank & Audrey."

The Lovesick Blues

Obviously, they could live neither with each other nor without. The "divorce" became final on the last week of May, but actually they had been merely separated for a few weeks—Audrey down there on the farm, Hank failing miserably to keep himself together in Montgomery—before they reunited at Lillie's boardinghouse and suddenly, voilà, were traipsing off to sunny Norfolk on what amounted to the honeymoon they had never gotten around to the first time. If anybody was being true to Hank's cause, it was the beleaguered Fred Rose, who, on the day he got that postcard, had already begun devising a plan. It was a given that Hank had to get out of Montgomery now, not later, or else be forever consigned to small-time glory at WSFA. The Opry was but a distant dream and would remain so until Hank produced a hit so big that they could deny him no longer, drunk or sober. Just as Audrey had shown her husband how to make it in Nashville, by going through the back door as a songwriter, Rose was mulling over a similar scheme for his boy to shorten his route to the stage of the Grand Ole Opry at Ryman Auditorium.

Rose thought he saw the answer for Hank in Shreveport, Louisiana, at KWKH, a 50,000-watt radio station that had just premiered a Saturday night jamboree fashioned after the Opry. They were calling it the Louisiana Hayride, a live four-hour show that could be heard over much of the eastern United

States, wherever it wasn't being blown off the air by the megapowered Mexican border stations booming up from the Rio Grande. Due to the sheer power of its own signal, KWKH had much the same clout in what the marketers called the Ark-La-Tex area as WSM did east of the Mississippi. Performers were pouring in from the vast countryside to play the Hayride, hoping the exposure would lead to an invitation to join the Opry. The people running the station and the Hayride weren't nearly as savvy and forward-looking as the insurance barons at WSM, and thus were content to serve as a feeder of talent to the well-established Opry. They called it the Cradle of the Stars, and indeed it would serve as the last stop before the major leagues for scores of superstars including Elvis Presley and Johnny Cash.

In spite of the success of "Move It On Over," which eventually peaked at No. 4 on the *Billboard* charts, placing Hank on the Hayride wasn't going to be easy. "Hank *who*?" would have been a plausible response from KWKH. The guy was a big-time drunk among drunks, they could say, and his success on a drowsy 1,000-watt station in south Alabama meant little to them. First, Rose took care of Hank by agreeing to put him on a fifty-dollar-a-month draw, an advance against royalties, and then he began calling in his chits from old friends at the station. He went to work on Dean Upson, commercial manager at KWKH, a fellow member of the Vagabonds when Fred found Nashville and broke away from the group. That led him to Horace Logan, the man in charge of the Hayride, who proposed that if Hank could stay sober for six months and prove it they would give him a shot. "Hank called me every week," Logan wrote in his memoirs, "and invariably he would have the manager of [WSFA] with him. 'Hank has been sober, he's been here every morning, he hasn't missed a single morning. He's sober as a judge,' and Hank'd say, 'That's right, I'm sober.'" He was anything but, of course, in that spring of his deepest angst, but the ploy was working. What probably nailed it was a weekend trip Hank and Audrey made to Shreveport in mid-summer, when Hank presented himself to the bosses and later hung out at a diner across the hall from the KWKH studios with some of the Hayride performers: chewing the fat, bitching about low pay, generally showing that he was one of the boys.

Hank signed off at WSFA for the last time in the waning days of July 1948, and he and Audrey (with Lycrecia, now seven years old) were on their way to Shreveport in a Chrysler sedan with mattresses and box springs strapped to the roof. They rented a garage apartment there and, once again, tried to settle in like any normal couple. Hank's deal with KWKH called for a fifty-dollar-a-week salary. He would host a fifteen-minute show at 5:15 every weekday morning, just him and his guitar, and perform on the Hayride most Saturday nights. He assembled a band, of a sort, the only member of the Drifting Cowboys willing to follow him to Shreveport being Lum York, the bass-thumping comic, but even that lasted only a few weeks. (Don Helms, the steel guitarist he wanted most, had a family and too good a gig at a skating rink in Andalusia to chance the move.) It would be tough going, financially, until Hank built a following in this new neck of the woods, and that began to happen the very moment he made his debut on the Louisiana Hayride on the first Saturday night in August. He was scheduled right after Johnnie and Jack, a duo who had also been placed there by Fred Rose, and when somebody backstage apologized for making him follow such a popular act, Hank shrugged it off with the comment, "I'll eat 'em alive." The packed house of 3,800 at the Municipal Auditorium, slightly larger than the capacity at the Opry's Ryman Auditorium, was slow to respond at first when he came onstage to do "Move It On Over," but when he had finished they were on their feet. After he and Audrey came out to sing "I Want to Live and Love" to lesser applause, he was done for the night.

Hank's contract didn't require him to appear on the Hayride each and every Saturday night, but he knew he would have to if he wanted this move to pay off. Within a month, he was picking up dates at schoolhouses and auditoriums and honky-tonks in northern Louisiana and eastern Texas, putting together various versions of the Cowboys as he went along, and soon he found a sponsor for his morning radio show: Johnnie Fair Syrup, a modest local family operation that aspired only to sell a few bottles of syrup. It turned out to be a propitious marriage, great for the business and so good for Hank that the tapes of those shows would become rare collectors' items. He was in his element. Alone in the KWKH studios before daybreak, entertaining himself and a half-awake engineer, Hank ("the Ol' Syrup-Sopper") strummed and sang what he liked, wrapping his soothing country twang around tunes like the Sons of the Pioneers' "Cool Water" as though staging a private concert for the farm families just beginning their day. Between songs he pitched syrup and his upcoming personal appearances, and at the close of the fifteen-minute show, as the sun was rising over Shreveport, he would pretend he was talking to a maid at his house: "Get the biscuits ready; I'm coming home and I need something to put my Johnnie Fair Syrup on." The show became so successful that the station began prerecording versions to be played when Hank was on the road.

Those first few months in Shreveport represented the one extended period of calm in the otherwise chaotic life of Hank Williams. Audrey not only was several hundred miles away from Lillie, but she had become pregnant and, as her belly swelled, was unable to perform onstage. Hank thoroughly enjoyed having Lycrecia around—the only reason he never formally adopted her was Audrey's fear that he would take her away in case of a divorce—and he was lulled by the idea of being part of a cozy family unit. Sober, relatively happy at home, quickly becoming the best-known performer on KWKH and at the Hayride, he happily rode off in his new Packard limousine (likened to a "stretch Dachsund") to play the road. "He was a great boss," said Clent Holmes, a guitarist who often accompanied him. "If I told him I couldn't reach a certain note, he'd say, 'Don't worry about it, hoss, just stomp your foot and smile.'" There were always fishing poles in the car, prompting Hank to stop any time he saw a likely pond, lake, or stream. Once, with Holmes driving, they came upon a hitchhiking hobo and Hank ordered Clent to stop. "We're full up and can't take you anywhere, friend," Hank told the man, "but here's some money so you can buy some food." (The way he spread the wealth when he had it, you can be sure he didn't just give the fellow a couple of dollar bills.) Hank had slipped into his repertoire a yodeling version of an old orphan of a show tune called "Lovesick Blues," sending crowds wild and, for the first time in his experience, teenaged girls were treating him like a country Frank Sinatra: after a show at an auditorium in Corpus Christi, Texas, a gaggle of them came after him with razor blades, intent on cutting off his necktie or a hank of clothing as a souvenir, even letting the air out of his tires to keep him from leaving. He was becoming as easygoing onstage as he was in the studio. "Ladies and gentlemen, to a country boy like me it makes you feel real good when people like a song you wrote," he would say, "like this one I'm fixin' to sing for you right now." There would be the cornpone patter with Lum York, the bass-playing comedian: "Well, let me ask you, if they had to graft some skin when your face got tore up in a car wreck, where'd they graft it from?" Lum: "Let's just say sometimes my face gets tired and wants to sit down." Except when working a roadhouse, there was always a hymn to be sung ("You boys gather around here now and let's do this old gospel song"). And, always, there was the familiar closing he used on the radio show: "If the good Lord's willin' and the creek don't rise, we'll see y'all Friday night at the Jasper High School auditorium." When he got home, his pockets full of money, he would kiss his wife and check out how the baby was coming.

The downside was this: Hank was so happy that he couldn't write a word. There had been some half-assed attempts as he rode along in the backseat with Clent Holmes and Lum York— "He tried a title on me once," said Holmes, "called 'Swimming a River of Blood,' and when I told him it was an awful title he never finished"—but the fire was gone. Life was *too* good. With steady work, money in the bank, and a peaceful home to come to, what wasn't to like? He had no complaints. Everything in life was fine, steady, downright *comfortable*; enough to make one think Ol' Hank might up and join the Kiwanis Club or the Rotarians. One couldn't help but think of Ernest Hemingway's pronouncements about the creative process: "In going where you have to go, and doing what you have to do, and seeing what you have to see, you dull and blunt the instrument you write with. But I would rather have it bent and dull and know I had to put it on the grindstone again and hammer it into

shape and put a whetstone to it, than to have it bright and shining and nothing to say, or smooth and well-oiled in the closet,
but unused." Hank had found happiness, and it didn't suit
him. The anger was gone. It was as though he couldn't write
without being mad about something. The instrument he used—
his heart and soul—was bright and shining, smooth and well-
oiled, and he had nothing to say.

The silence had so puzzled Fred Rose that he sent his promotion man, Mel Foree, out to Shreveport to check up on Hank.
Acuff-Rose and MGM had been releasing a new Hank
Williams record about once a month during the recording ban
by the musicians' union—"I'm a Long Gone Daddy" had
peaked at No. 6 during its three weeks on the *Billboard* chart,
but nothing much had happened with "I Saw the Light," "Pan
American," "Honky Tonkin'," and the others—and the well
was about dry. Hank seemed glad to see somebody from the
home office, and Foree dutifully went on the road with him for
a few dates before reporting that things were going well with
Hank—*too* well, he noted—and then nudged him into making
demos of some new songs the two had worked on together.
When the package of demos arrived on Fred's desk in
Nashville, he broke out in a clammy sweat. It was crap, pure
crap, as far as he was concerned; especially the one called
"Lovesick Blues," a borrowed tune one year older than Hank
himself, which was out of meter, had no bridge, and was full of
difficult chord changes. Time was running short. Due to the
recording ban, Hank hadn't been in a studio for more than a
year, when they had cut those eight tunes back in November of
'47. How they were going to advance Hank's career with this
mess was inconceivable, but they had to have *something* new.

Fred booked a three-hour session at a recording studio in Cincinnati—the E. T. Herzog Studio—simply because that was home base for Red Foley's Opry band, the ones he wanted for the session. They gathered there three days before Christmas of 1948.

Shouting matches erupted in the studio before the musicians even had time to uncrate and tune their instruments. It was all about "Lovesick Blues." Hank had been performing the song since his days in south Alabama, had experienced the wild reactions of audiences everywhere from Thigpen's Log Cabin in Georgiana to the meanest roadhouses in the piney woods of the violent Big Thicket area of east Texas, and he was adamant about putting it on a record. When he was advised that the original first verse ("I'm in love, I'm in love, with a beautiful gal") was being used as a chorus, and the original chorus ("I've got a feeling called the blues") was being used as an opening verse, Hank didn't know what they were talking about. "I'll tell you one damn thing," he yelled at Rose, remembering the packs of teenaged girls rushing to tear his clothes off after he had performed it in Texas, "you might not like the song, but when I walk off the stage and throw my hat back on the stage and the *hat* encores, that's pretty hot." Never were their artistic differences clearer—Fred was a musical technician, a stickler for symmetry, while the untutored Hank couldn't write a note but understood the raw emotions in a song because he had lived them—and Fred responded by repeating what a disaster he felt the song represented, finally saying he wasn't going to have anything to do with it. The musicians stood aside while the debate raged, but they didn't like the tune, either: "That's the worst damn thing I ever heard," whispered steel guitarist Jerry Byrd, who later would record

with Rosemary Clooney, Patti Page, Jimmy Wakely, and Jimmy
Dean, but on this day had never even heard of Hank Williams.

And so they went to work. The only one of the four songs
that Fred Rose truly approved of was a classic Hank tune
about a guy whose true love has wed another, "There'll Be No
Teardrops Tonight," but the others were a pair of duets with
Audrey and, of course, "Lovesick Blues." If anyone had ever
doubted how truly awful Audrey's singing voice could be, they
got a screeching earful when she and Hank teamed up on
"Lost on the River" and "I Heard My Mother Praying for Me."
She yowled, jumped in whenever she felt like it, and practically drowned out the voice of a husband who one day would
become the quintessential country singer. Whether they knew
it or not, those in the studio that day were bearing witness to
the ongoing battle that had raged between Hank and Audrey
for all of those years: not a collaboration but a competition between the two. (None of this was lost, by the way, on the
Hayride's Horace Logan: "Audrey was a pure, unmitigated,
hard-boiled, blue-eyed bitch. She wanted to be a singer and
she was horrible, unbelievably horrible. She not only tried to
sing, she *insisted* on it, and she forced herself on stage when
Hank was out there. I'd never let her go out, but Hank would
say, 'Logan, I've got to let her sing. I've got to live with the
woman.'" Logan solved it during performances on the Hayride
with two microphones: a live one for Hank, a dead one for Audrey.) After they had put down "Teardrops" and the duets, with
about half an hour of studio time remaining, they revisited the
question of recording "Lovesick Blues."

With Rose fuming behind the glass, Hank was down on the
floor of the studio strumming his guitar and going through the
opening strains of the song for the studio musicians, restating

his case. "It's a yodel thing," Jerry Byrd was explaining to
Zeke Turner, the electric guitarist, before asking Hank where
the break would come. "When you see me do this," Hank said,
nodding his head and stomping his foot. Byrd said, "Hank,
that's terrible. You ain't going to put this thing out, are you?"
Shrugging, eager to get on with it, Hank told him, "It don't
make any difference. We've got the ones we want, anyhow.
This is just the 'B' side or something." Rose had heard
enough. "Look, Hank, if you insist on doing this, you go ahead
and put it on, but I'm not going to stay and listen to it. I'm going to go get a cup of coffee." As he was headed out the door
he shouted to the musicians that he would pay them time-and-
a-half if they finished the cut before the remaining ten minutes
ran out. Hank knew that studio costs would come out of his
royalties. "You're mighty damn free with my money!" he yelled
at Fred's back.

Like it or not, the band had the record Hank wanted after
only two takes, just under the wire. "Well, what you got?" Rose
said when he returned to the studio, back from having his cup
of coffee. The engineer played the cut. Hank was pleased, and
the backup musicians were at least relieved that they had successfully negotiated the intricate rhythms and chord changes.
"My God, Hank," said Fred, "I still say that's the worst thing
I've ever heard."

Fred and Wesley Rose had to track down the publishing infor-
mation before MGM could release "Lovesick Blues," and they
ran into a hornet's nest. Hank didn't help things when he told
them he had bought the rights from an Alabama performer
named Rex Griffin, even owned a copy of Griffin's Decca
recording from 1939, but what he really meant was that the two

of them got drunk together and Hank paid a few bucks to "borrow" Griffin's arrangement. The one thing certain was that the song had been around for a very long time and hadn't succeeded for anybody. It had been first recorded as a bluesy number in 1922, by several artists, and then showed up in a musical about lovesick airmen, *O-oo Ernest,* that never made it as far as off-Broadway. At that time authorship was given to Irving Mills for the lyrics and Cliff Friend for the melody—Mills had been a force behind Duke Ellington's music, Friend a down-and-out vaudevillian—and so they were the two who ultimately shared writing credits when Hank's version was released in February of '49. Whatever. Hank was the one man who had found the core of the song, the absolute despair of a man whose woman has left him at the end of his rope, and he yodeled it with such emotion that you would think he was going to drop dead on the spot from a broken heart. He had ridden this wild bull of a song and tamed it.

Although Fred would never get over his misreading of "Lovesick," he certainly enjoyed the money it brought in. Hank's recording sold forty-eight thousand copies in the first two weeks of its life in the stores, made the country charts after one month, and within three months—in the May 7, 1949, issue of *Billboard*—it had dislodged George Morgan's saccharine pop song "Candy Kisses" at the top of the charts. Hank found that out while having lunch at the Bantam Grill, the hangout near the KWKH studios favored by Hayride performers. "I'd bought a *Billboard* at the newsstand [and] walked in and I showed it to him," said Tillman Franks, a songwriter and performer who had begun booking Hank's appearances. "It shook him up pretty good. He just sat there silent the longest time. He realized what that meant." Later in the day, as a

means of dealing with the idea that he might be on his way to
stardom, Hank was adopting his usual *aw-shucks* routine: "I
sure am glad it ain't another damn 'Pontchartrain.'" His
"Lovesick Blues" remained No. 1 for four months, and was
still hanging around on the charts in January of the following
year. In the order of things in those days, the Grand Ole Opry
couldn't be far behind for Hank, but in the bigger picture there
was this to consider: a sweet little ditty like "Candy Kisses,"
more pop than country ("candy kisses, wrapped in paper,
mean more to you than any of mine"), had been kicked aside
by an anguished *cri de coeur*. A baton was about to be passed
from one generation of country singers to quite another breed.

Despite his misgivings about the quality of "Lovesick,"
Rose had arranged two more recording sessions for Hank in
March of '49 in order to have plenty in MGM's can just in case.
Hank had been so dry for so long that he had little to offer in
the way of fresh material of his own—the only "keepers" were
"Mind Your Own Business" and "You're Gonna Change (Or
I'm Gonna Leave)," both written when his times were more
desperate, which is to say more fertile for him as a writer—but
the sessions paid off, nevertheless, thanks to songs by other
writers, tunes that he so personalized that, like "Lovesick,"
hard-core Hank fans would insist that they were his very own.
One of them was "Wedding Bells," credited to one Claude
Boone but actually written by a drunk who had sold it to Boone
for twenty-five dollars to keep the booze flowing (odd, how often that happened in those days). The other was "Lost Highway," written by a blind singer out of Houston by the name of
Leon Payne. "Wedding Bells" may have been just another
maudlin weeper, with lines that might have come from one of
Hank and Audrey's romance magazines ("a blossom from an

orange tree in your hair"), but by the time Hank was done with it the song rode piggyback with "Lovesick" to No. 2 on the charts and ultimately earned $40,000 for Claude Boone, the "writer," a fine return on his $25 investment. As for "Lost Highway," Hank claimed it for himself by putting the lyrics in the first person, and Fred Rose once again reworked it to soften his client's references to booze and sin: "Just a woman's lies and a jug of gin / Sent me down this road of sin" became a "deck of cards" and a "jug of wine," rhyming with "a life like mine."

The ringing success of "Lovesick Blues" wrought remarkable changes in Hank's life and career almost overnight. The Louisiana Hayride had a genuine superstar on its hands for the first time and was making full use of him. When the Shreveport Chamber of Commerce put together a unique whistle-stop tour of southern Louisiana and Texas by train, pausing at depots and crossroads and even remote "pig trails," Hank closed each stop by singing two songs and autographing everything in sight before the train chugged away. Nobody wanted to follow him onstage anymore, whether in Shreveport or on the road. He was getting clamorous encores whenever he performed "Lovesick," and every time Hank announced a gospel was forthcoming, the house lights were dimmed and up came a spotlight at Municipal Auditorium. Pumped and full of himself, he took to backing away as the audience roared, tipping his hat and mouthing words that only the nearest band member could hear: "Ain't it a shame, ain't it a shame, ain't it a shame." His pockets were stuffed with dollar bills, almost like "found" money, from cash sales of autographed records, photographs, and songbooks everywhere he played. He hired a full-time band and put them on salary, bought a trailer to haul the equipment behind the Packard (unable to get the hang of it, he had to have a band member back it into the driveway for him), and he bought a house in a subdivision across the Red River in Bossier City. On the verge of making the really big money, he hired as a full-time manager one of the best in the business, Oscar Davis, the dapper, foul-mouthed, overbearing vaudeville promoter who had introduced country music to New York City with a concert at Carnegie Hall. He even took his first plane ride, for that second session at Castle Studio in March of that year, wiring Rose that morning: "Flight 58 will arrive 545 I hope."

And he was drinking again, no thanks to Audrey. She had ridden with Hank to Nashville to duet with him on the two gospel numbers in early March, but that would be the penultimate time she would ever record with him. Pregnant now, more irritable than ever, she was not amused by the success Hank was having without her at his side. He would buy jewelry for her, and she would throw it in his face. He would bring home a set of crystal to celebrate the new house, and she would shatter it by flinging it onto the carport. He got into the beer during a picnic for Hayride people, and when he got home, late and drunk, Audrey took an ice pick to the tires of his car. Hank didn't know which way to turn: en route to a date in Lake Charles with band members Felton Pruett and Lum York, they had to stop at a doctor's office to repair Pruett's nose, bloodied and broken by one of Hank's errant bony knees during a scuffle in the car. "The only thing he really wanted was to be loved," said Mamie Holmes, Clent's wife, who baby-sat Audrey during her pregnancy while Hank was out of town, "but she was as needy as he was." Often Hank showed up for shows with battle scars on his face. He got to where he couldn't wait to get back on the road, away from Audrey and into the arms of his ebullient, adoring fans. The raucous hard-drinking Cajun crowds he met in southern Louisiana loved everything about him: this rawboned, hungry, cocky hillbilly who seemed to be living a hard life and writing about it as it happened. Little wonder that, years later, when Hank wrote and recorded "Jambalaya," they accepted it as a sort of love letter from one of their own: "Pick guitar, fill fruit jar, and be gay-o / Son of a gun we'll have big fun on the bayou . . . ."

And then, finally, the Opry beckoned.

Not for nothing did they call Ryman Auditorium the Mother Church of Country Music. The Grand Ole Opry itself had originated in 1925, the idea of George D. Hay, a former Memphis newspaperman, who was hired as program manager for WSM only a month after the station's founding. Sensing sales opportunities for the National Life & Accident Insurance Company, owners of WSM, Hay propped up an old mountain fiddler named Uncle Jimmy Thompson in front of a carbon microphone in the station's studio and had him saw away for more than an hour on a Saturday night in November of '25. He came up with a name for the program one night following the end of the NBC network's weekly showcase of classical music: "For the past hour we have been listening to music largely from grand opera, but from now on we will present 'grand ole opree.'" (For years, Hay, now referring to himself as "the Solemn Old Judge," opened the show by blowing on a steamboat whistle and ominously intoning, "Let 'er go, boys," opening the floodgates for a procession of fiddlers, singers, and clog dancers.) The Opry wandered from one venue to another until 1941, when it was moved to Ryman Auditorium in downtown

Nashville. A fierce redbrick two-story building with stained-glass windows and semicircular rows of severe church pews, sitting five blocks up the hill from the Cumberland River at the end of Broadway, the Ryman was the legacy of a freewheeling riverboat captain named Thomas Ryman, who had been brought to his knees by a tent-show evangelist's sermon on motherhood, saw the light, threw all of the booze and gambling paraphernalia on his boat into the river, and built a tabernacle to honor the evangelist and the Lord.

To the performers and their fans, the Opry was Yankee Stadium without the grandeur. Ryman Auditorium had been built before the turn of the century, and by the forties she had the aura of an antebellum mansion gone to seed. The cramped dressing rooms barely afforded space to turn around in; the worn wooden church pews were hardly cushy; nurses patrolled the balcony in those pre–air conditioning days, looking for heatstroke victims; a man might as well go out and pee in the alleyway as hope to find a respectable restroom; bulky hand-painted flats were lowered to form backdrops for the stage, one replacing another as each half-hour portion's sponsor changed (from Prince Albert tobacco to Union overalls to Goo-Goo candy bars). It was, after all, primarily a radio show that went out over WSM to nearly half of the United States. (An apocryphal story deals with a farmer who has been listening to the Opry for years as its signal crackled in and out; when he gets back home, having finally made it to the Ryman for a live performance, he marvels to report the one thing that truly impressed him: "There wadn't no static.") Serpentine lines circled the auditorium, roiling with fans who had driven an average of five hundred miles, tired but giddy, craning for a peek at typewritten listings, framed and posted like restaurant menus on the heavy front doors, to see if their favorites would be performing that night. Paying their eighty cents at the door, they grabbed free funeral-parlor fans and clamored for the choicest seats, and then began popping flashbulbs as the stars began parading across the scarred and musty stage in their gaudy Western-cut costumes, like matadors wearing sequined suits of light.

Oscar Davis and Fred Rose had been lobbying WSM to give Hank a guest spot on the Opry, a performer's first step toward becoming a full-time member if all went well. Oscar promised a year of sobriety in Hank's behalf, and Fred bribed the Opry's two top managers with shares of the writing credit for a song he had written, "Chattanoogie Shoe Shine Boy," which would become No. 1 the following year. When they finally got a date—Saturday night, June 11, 1949—Hank was momentarily distracted. Two weeks earlier, on May 25 (the first anniversary of the divorce that never happened), Audrey had given birth to a boy they named Randall Hank Williams; a whopping ten-pounder who "like to killed the both of us," Audrey said, adding that nurses had to hold Hank down when he heard her screaming during the delivery. He had sent another wire to Rose—"10 lb boy borned this morning at 145. Both doeing fine"—and whimsically nicknamed his son Bocephus, the name Rod Brasfield, Roy Acuff's comic, had given to his stage dummy. He had to borrow $100 from the boys at the Bantam Grill to help pay the hospital and doctor's bills. He signed off at KWKH with a rousing performance of "Lovesick Blues" that drew seven encores, a record that Horace Logan would never allow to be broken. Having cleared the base, as it were, Hank was on his way to the big time now, knowing that at least when he embarked on the trip to Nashville for the biggest moment in any country singer's life, Audrey would be nursing the baby, too preoccupied to bitch about being left behind.

In the eight decades since the founding of the Opry, untold thousands of performers have made their debut—the first step toward stardom for some, but for the vast majority three minutes to be remembered before they returned to oblivion— but only one debut has been memorialized. When the show was moved to a new venue far from downtown Nashville, the bosses at WSM were wise enough to have a huge circle of wood cut from the stage at Ryman Auditorium and have it implanted—*The Exact Spot Where Hank Williams Made His Debut!*—at the spacious, carpeted, air-conditioned Grand Ole Opry House, giving further pause to any hillbilly wannabe who wasn't nervous enough already. It was that kind of night.

Like a lone gunman, a stranger headed to town, Hank had driven the six hundred miles from Shreveport to Nashville and checked into the Hermitage Hotel on Friday afternoon so he would be rested. Toward dusk on Saturday, he locked the doors of his Packard in the gravel parking lot behind the Ryman, trundled down the hill to the stage-door entrance, signed in like everybody else, and entered the madhouse that was the backstage area on any Opry night. Fred Rose was there to greet him, along with Oscar Davis and a couple of WSM's big-wigs, and Hank knew some of the stars from older times—Red Foley, Ernest Tubb, Roy Acuff, Minnie Pearl, Little Jimmy Dickens—but for the most part he was just another old boy in cowboy boots and a Stetson, carrying a guitar case. He had gotten there in time to watch and listen to the Opry's prime-time show, sponsored by Prince Albert tobacco and hosted by the smooth-talking Foley, which was picked up by NBC and aired to 150 stations and ten million listeners throughout the nation; a program deemed so vital by the Opry and the network that it was scripted right down to the second and fully rehearsed earlier in the day. When that portion ended at nine o'clock, up went the Prince Albert backdrop and down came the flats advertising Warren Paints, the signal for Tubb and his Texas Troubadours to hit the stage.

While "E. T.," as Tubb was known, broke into "I'm Walkin' the Floor over You," Hank hovered in the shadows with the pickup band that would back him on his debut. If he was nervous, he didn't show it. "Williams, you're next," said a fellow holding a clipboard, the Opry's stage manager. As Tubb sang the closing refrain of "Walkin' the Floor," there was a rustle among the entertainers backstage, veteran stars and sidemen alike. "C'mon, y'all gotta hear this guy," said Billy Robinson, who would back Hank on the steel guitar, and many of the Opry regulars closed in. They had heard of his performances, knew of the baggage he carried, and they were curious. Tubb finished his turn at the microphone, there was a commercial for Warren Paints, and then Cousin Louie Buck, the WSM announcer standing stage right and reading from a script, made the introduction: *Making his debut on the Opry ... that Lovesick boy ... a great big Warren Paints welcome ... Hank Williams!!*

There was some spontaneous applause, urged on by Cousin Louie's waving his hands for more as Hank's gaunt form suddenly loomed in the spotlight—a twenty-five-year-old who appeared older and taller than his six-one and 150 pounds—and the crowd of 3,500 didn't need any more prompting when they heard the familiar opening strains of "Lovesick Blues." *Oh, so that's the guy.* They never really knew what had hit them.

> *I got a feeling called the blues, oh, Lord,*
> *Since my baby said good-bye,*
> *Lord, I don't know what I'll do-ooo-ooo*
> *All I do is sit and sigh-ee-yi-ee-yi-yiii . . .*

It had been one thing to hear the song over the radio, but quite another to see him perform it in person. He was so skinny that when he leaned into the WSM microphone and began to sway with the rhythm, his legs appeared to dangle as though he were a marionette on strings. The yowling yodel of *sigh-ee-yi-ee-yi-yiii* brought almost everybody in the house to their feet—absolutely stunned—and the rush to the stage was on. Flashbulbs lit up the Ryman like Christmas tree lights. Young women stumbled all over each other to take his snapshot and get a closer look, hoping to be the one he chose to pick out of the crowd; older women simply wanted to take him home for a good meal, put some meat on those bones, and tell him everything was going to be all right. Even the Opry veterans in the wings were howling, back-slapping, rolling their eyes, gaping.

> *And I'm oh so lonesome,*
> *I've got the lovesick blues . . .*

He strummed the final chord, bowed, tipped his hat, and began backing away from the near-hysterical crowd—*Ain't it a shame, ain't it a shame, ain't it a shame*—but they wouldn't let

him go. He came back to give them more . . . and more . . . and
more. Cousin Louie Buck had a radio show to run, a time
schedule to follow, and he tried to stop them—

She'll do me, she'll do you
  She's got that kind of lovin'
Lord I love to hear her when she calls me sweet daddy,
  Such a beautiful dream . . .

—but they wouldn't quit. Many thousands of fans claiming
they were there, ten times the actual capacity of the Ryman,
are still swearing Hank did six encores of "Lovesick Blues"
that night. That never happened, exactly, but it's beside the
point. The fact is, you couldn't tell where one "encore" ended
and another began. Suffice it to say that there was a continuous
uproar during his entire performance, nearly ten minutes of
bedlam, and that the Opry had never seen anything like it before, or since. Two hours later, when Hank sang "Move It on
Over" during the eleven o'clock Allen Manufacturing show, he
was welcomed back to the stage as though he were already an
Opry regular.

A Star Is Born

Royalty from the very beginning, Hank was whisked back the very next weekend for a spot on the networked Prince Albert portion of the Opry. This time he was flown in from Shreveport, like a bona fide star, went through the rehearsal on the morning of the show, lolled around the hotel all afternoon, and got a proper introduction that night from Red Foley, who asked for "a rousing Prince Albert welcome to the 'Lovesick Blues' boy, Hank Williams." In the scripted chatter that followed, Foley said he hoped "you'll be here for a long, long time, buddy," a tacit announcement that he had already been accepted into the Opry family. "Well, Red," Hank drawled, "it looks like I'll be doing just that, and I'll be looking forward to it." And here came "Lovesick Blues" again, with much the same audience reaction, except now he was being heard by ten million people hunkered around radios throughout North America and into Canada. Hiram Williams, Lillie and Lon's boy, had reached the pinnacle of country music at the age of twenty-five. Nobody had ever made it faster to the top.

To be added to the official roster of the Opry was the ultimate endorsement for a country music performer. Although some stars over the years would turn down the opportunity, on the grounds that they could do better by playing big-ticket concerts in major cities rather than hustling back to work the cramped Ryman for peanuts on the biggest night of the week, most would kill to be an Opry regular. There were about four dozen of them when Hank was accepted to the club, which was exactly what it was, and the benefits far outweighed the losses. A star would be showcased twice over the course of a Saturday night at the Opry, performing as many as a half dozen songs for a radio audience representing the most faithful of country listeners all over the nation, and the biggest names like Hank and Acuff might make a third appearance on a live show broadcast from Ernest Tubb's Record Shop around the corner from the Ryman. The radio exposure, not the minimal pay, made it worthwhile to interrupt a tour, dash back to Nashville, do the Opry, and then leave immediately to resume the tour. Regulars were obliged to make at least twenty-six appearances on the Opry each year, and in exchange for that they could advertise themselves as a "star of the Grand Ole Opry" wherever they went. They were also offered the clout of WSM's Artist Service Bureau, ruled by a bearish company man named Jim Denny, who, for a percentage of the take, put together concerts and tours.

From all appearances, Hank had finally found a home and was ready to settle down for the long haul. He was a father now, and a stepfather, and he and Audrey were shopping around for a house in Nashville. He had just signed a fresh contract with MGM Records, which suddenly had a cash cow on its hands and was making the most of it by releasing records as fast as Hank could cut them. His relationship with Fred Rose was turning into a dream collaboration between a raw storyteller and a slick tunesmith, neatly summarized in a simple sentence by Mitch Miller, the Columbia record producer who would later place many of Hank's songs on the pop charts: "Every good writer needs a good editor." For a personal manager he had the indefatigable Oscar Davis, the man who had brazenly introduced live country music to New York. He had even found a Nashville banker he could trust, a fellow named Sam Hunt, who delighted in allowing Hank to play the laid-back cowboy; coming in from a week of playing one-nighters on the road, Hank would amble into the bank when it opened on a Monday and begin emptying pockets crammed with crumpled bills and personal checks onto the counter, telling a bemused cashier, "I make it, you count it." In that summer of '49, suddenly thrust upon the world, Hank had it made. He was sober, his records were selling, his voice could be heard all across the land, and he was about to unleash the greatest single portfolio of songs ever written by any one person in the history of country music.

Now Hank could stop taking no for an answer from the men he had wanted for years to have as a part of the Drifting Cowboys. At the very top of his list was Don Helms, the steel guitarist from rural south Alabama, whose history with Hank dated back to playing at Thigpen's Log Cabin. The steel was the most important element in Hank's accompaniment, a delicate echo of his mournful cry when played properly, and Helms had the perfect touch. When he said yes to Hank, the others followed: Jerry Rivers, a sprightly young fiddler, son of a Miami dentist, who had served an apprenticeship with an offshoot of Tubb's Texas Troubadours; bass player Hillous Butrum; and guitarist Bob McNett. All of them were slightly younger than Hank, healthy and hungry and eager to see more of America, veterans already of the hard life out there on the road. Putting together the right band was an imperative for Hank this time around, after too many years of having to tell virtual strangers to come in on the chorus "when you see me stomp," and he had learned the hard way the necessity of teamwork and simple compatibility for a group of men faced with hours cramped together in an automobile for days on end. They understood the basic simplicity of Hank's music and their role in it ("Keep it vanilla," was all he asked.). He paid them salaries slightly above the average, and sometimes they could double that from the cut they got from hawking photos, songbooks, and records to audiences. The group began to coalesce after only a couple of loose jam sessions—Hank became "Harm" and "Bones," Helms with his long hair was nicknamed "Shag," and Rivers's crew cut cried out for "Burrhead"—and they were quickly okayed by the Opry's Jim Denny, who could have insisted on a house band if he had found them lacking. They would become the most famous Drifting Cowboys ever. Something big was about to happen, and Jerry Rivers could feel it from the start: "As we rolled out of Nashville in Hank's long, blue Packard after my first Opry appearance with Hank, I sat quietly in the back knowing I had changed. In those few moments on stage, watching Hank perform and watching the audience respond, I regained a humility I'd lost somewhere along the way."

Rolling away from the Ryman at midnight on a Saturday, pulling a little aluminum trailer with *Hank Williams & the Drifting Cowboys* hand-painted on its side, they went in search of their fortunes. The road was their mistress. Like the long-haul truckers they would pass in the night, they were constantly searching for country music or baseball games on the radio, not to mention keeping eyes peeled for gas stations and truck stops; dodging drunk drivers and highway patrolmen; trying to sleep; and wondering when they might take a decent shower again. Often they covered four hundred miles between shows. Once, a buzzard came flying through the windshield. More than once, they ran out of gas. Another time, a jerry-built gizmo somebody had devised as a precursor of air-conditioning, a bullet-shaped intake lodged in the partly opened window and filled with excelsior and alcohol, suddenly went haywire, giving them an acrid bath they hadn't anticipated. They were playing better venues now, bigger places in bigger towns like Dallas and St. Louis, but they weren't averse to working from the roofs of concessions stands at drive-in theaters. "What rhymes with 'street'?" Hank would holler, riding shotgun, pencil poised over his schoolboy's composition notebook, and from the back would come a yelp from Don Helms: "Your smelly feet!" Hank was so bad about cadging cigarettes that he would mindlessly reach into another's shirt pocket to bum one, a practice that ended when one of the Cowboys found some exploding cigarettes at a novelty shop. They were on such a natural high, living a dream, that nobody was drinking so much as a beer, including Hank.

You would think that Fred Rose would be beside himself with joy by now, seeing Hank's career take off like that, but he seemed to be lagging behind as though he couldn't quite believe it. He had badly underestimated the power of "Lovesick Blues"—hadn't even wanted to record it, in fact—and he was still having reservations when Hank pulled into Cincinnati for another session at Herzog Studio as the summer ended. For starters, Fred still didn't think the Drifting Cowboys were ready for prime time and so he made them stand around and merely listen in the studio while the core of the band from the "Lovesick" session, most noticeably the more gossamer steel guitarist Jerry Byrd, played backup. Fred liked two of the songs Hank offered—"I Just Don't Like This Kind of Livin'" and "A House without Love"—but not the others. Especially troublesome was a bluesy number called "My Bucket's Got a Hole in It," which many would swear Hank had first heard from Tee-Tot Payne as a kid, but actually was a tune that had been floating around in African American jazz and blues circles since the thirties. Here, again, Fred was concerned for the sake of Hank's image; specifically, a line reading "I can't buy no beer." ("Bucket" is the only recording where Hank can be heard playing solo, in an acoustic guitar riff.) The other was a song that Hank had first envisioned as a recitation—"I'm So Lonesome I Could Cry"—before deciding at the last minute to put it to music. With the newly appointed Cowboys morosely standing by in the studio, and Hank and Fred done with their squabbling, they got down to cutting the records. As it turned out when they were released, Fred was wrong again: "Bucket" hit No. 2 on the charts when it was released three months later, and "A House without Love" sank like a rock, although "This Kind of Livin'" topped out at No. 5. As for "I'm So Lonesome I Could Cry," the marvelously poetic dirge that Hank himself would call the favorite of all the songs he wrote, its fate would wind up in the hands of the historians. Rose had put it on the flip side of "Bucket," a mere afterthought, and—get this—the best it ever did on the charts was No. 43, in 1966, more than a dozen years after Hank's death, when a reappraisal of his work was under way. Never has so great a piece of songwriting been so egregiously overlooked.

Meanwhile, back at the ranch house Hank and Audrey had finally picked out, near the governor's mansion on Franklin Road in Nashville, Audrey was sending the ladies of the "Athens of the South" into apoplexy. Just as they had feared, the barbarians were, indeed, at the gate. Hank had paid

$21,000 for your basic three-bedroom redbrick cottage, the postwar "ranch" design beginning to sprout up all over the new American suburbs at the time, and Audrey had gotten out the checkbook. She would teach these old biddies to poke fun at "hillbillies." She would show them what real class looked like. At all hours of the day, and sometimes into the night, there was a steady hum of traffic up and down bucolic Franklin Road bringing tradesmen of every ilk: plumbers, carpenters, masons, electricians; designers, landscapers, lighting experts, sound technicians; burly men lugging brand-new chairs and tables and sofas and beds and rolls of lush carpeting. This was going to be . . . *amazing*! Oriental was her thing. Why, they could have luaus, those little Hawaiian parties where you wear leis and grass skirts and go barefoot, and maybe Don Helms could play some of that island music, you know; the steel guitar *is* a Hawaiian thingie, isn't it? . . . Before MGM could release Hank's record of "I Just Don't Like This Kind of Livin'," Audrey had transformed the house into a place where he was reluctant to sit down beneath the glassy chandeliers. Black lacquer and gold dragons dominated the décor, not to mention beaded curtains and rickety bamboo seats and faux waterfalls and a jukebox, and all of it was a way of saying that they—she, actually, Audrey Mae Sheppard of Pike County, Alabama— had made it. And wait until passersby got a load of the pièce de résistance: a wrought-iron railing across the front porch that displayed the opening chords of "Lovesick Blues."

With that kind of money going out the front door, it was a good thing Hank was bringing plenty of it in. A lot of the songs that had started slowly now were rising high in the charts on a tide lifted by "Lovesick." He was still second in record sales to

Eddy Arnold, "the Tennessee Plowboy," a velvety baritone more pop than country, but all of the talk in the business was of Hank. Now *this* is country, they were saying, while Arnold was just playing at it. Eddy belonged in a nightclub up east somewhere, in a tuxedo, with violins, not fiddles. Hank, on the other hand, came across as some old boy who really was a plowboy, headed at day's end for some beer joint to sing and play for the neighbors about his troubles. Country music, in fact, was beginning to expand and grow beyond its roots for the first time. Most of that was due to the outward migration of white southerners during the war years and afterward, when they carried their music with them to military posts around the world and to ports and factories all across the United States. You still had the Appalachian shouters and stompers, personified by Acuff with his fiddling and wailing about Mama and trains and sin. Tubb was sort of the eastern representative of Bob Wills and the Texas Playboys' western swing, with his Texas Troubadours and their signature dance tunes like "I'd Waltz across Texas with You." Arnold and George Morgan represented the new stuff—slick, smooth, dreamy, apropos of hardly anything in real life—and then there was Hank Williams. Hank wrote and sang as though he was running scared, which wasn't far from the truth. "Those fears are part of the talent," said Mitch Miller. "Who else could write 'How can I free your doubtful mind and melt your cold, cold heart'? That's a man who's really terribly afraid he's going to lose that woman. He was a shy man. The best way he could say it was in his songs." The public didn't know the half of it at that point, didn't know about the tragedy of Shakespearean proportions that the Hank-and-Audrey marriage was becoming, but they could sense it in his outpourings.

Since a major part of his education had come from listening
to WSFA as a kid, Hank was a natural on radio. Alone in a studio, he had a way of speaking quietly and confidentially to a
person at the other end, almost like a preacher offering conso-
lation: *Look, friend, I know exactly how you feel because I've
been there myself.* His skills had been sharpened during his
stint in Shreveport, cozying up to his unseen audience as "the
Ol' Syrup-Sopper" for Johnnie Fair Syrup, and WSM was
keeping him busy with similar shows for sponsors like Duck-
head overalls and Pops-Rite popcorn and Mother's Best flour.
(Hank was earning $100 a week to perform the fifteen-minute
Mother's Best shows, aired daily on WSM at 7:15 every morning, and the seventy-two recorded shows he left behind are
valued items today.) None of this was lost on one of the station's advertising managers. A state senator in Louisiana
named Dudley LeBlanc had concocted a classic "patent medicine" that he called Hadacol, its twelve percent alcohol base
being good for what ails you, especially if you lived in a legally
"dry" county, and he had become giddy with the possibilities
of advertising since cashing in on the rise to the charts of an
unsolicited tune entitled "Hadacol Boogie." LeBlanc remembered seeing Hank during his Shreveport days, and he was an
easy mark when the ad man at WSM proposed a syndicated radio show, starring Hank and Audrey, to be called "Health and
Happiness." The irony in the title was priceless, of course,
Hank never experiencing much of either in his lifetime, and he
used the programs to showcase the hymns and gospels he was
fond of singing almost in atonement for what Lillie and Audrey
regarded as his sins. There were eight shows in all, fifteen
minutes each, perfect for radio stations in the rural South's
Bible Belt to schedule on Sunday mornings. Hank and the

Cowboys taped them at WSM's studios on two successive Sun-
days in October of that year, and if Hank got anything out of it
besides the considerable money and more exposure it was yet
another heavy message that Audrey had to go; she jumped in
during the first session, to Dudley LeBlanc's chagrin, but was
so bad that she wasn't invited back for the second.

As more proof of the power behind being associated with
WSM and the Opry, Hank was invited to join a troupe that
would tour U.S. Air Force bases in Europe for two weeks in
November. He was in high cotton—the others were Opry veterans Foley, Acuff, Dickens, Minnie Pearl, and Rod Brasfield—
and they lumbered across the Atlantic in Gen. Dwight
Eisenhower's former private plane. Audrey was with them, as
were the other wives and WSM's top executives, as they
popped in on military hospitals and performed for the troops in
Frankfurt, Munich, Berlin, and Vienna. Country music was the
big ticket over Armed Forces Radio, its most popular program
being "Hillbilly Gasthaus," and huge crowds of soldiers and
German natives greeted them with waves of encores when
Hank sang "Lovesick Blues" and Foley did "Chattanoogie
Shoe Shine Boy." Two of the performances were taped and
played on the Prince Albert portion of the Opry. Surrounded
by fellow stars and the men who called the shots at the Opry,
Hank took pains to be on his best behavior, going so far as to
sniff glasses at the dinner table to make sure they held water
instead of wine. He may not have spent much time soaking up
European culture on his first trip away from the North American continent—he had his comic books for reading and insisted on slathering catsup on his cooked-to-death steaks—but
a good time was had by all. When he got back to Nashville,

"My Bucket's Got a Hole in It" was No. 2 with a bullet on the *Billboard* chart.

Then, for the first time during his employ at the Opry, he lost it. Oscar Davis had dropped all of his other clients to concentrate on Hank's career, and he had booked Hank and the Drifting Cowboys on an extensive tour of Canada and the Midwest that would wind down in Baltimore and Washington, D.C., just before Christmas. Oscar was an older man who reminded Don Helms of a New York dandy—short, stout, dapper in his crisp white shirts and good suits and pointy-toed black dress shoes—reminiscent of the old-school "drummers" who could sell anything to anybody. He had guaranteed WSM that Hank would stay sober for a year if they would put him on the Opry, but somewhere in the Midwest he began to see ominous signs of an impending disaster and hired a Pinkerton detective to travel along and keep his eye on Hank. Oscar had been in show business long enough to know that alcoholics are among the most cunning people on earth—when they want a drink they'll find one—but Hank beat anything he had ever seen. He had discovered that half-pint bottles and airline miniatures could easily be transported, in his guitar case or his cowboy boots or even beneath the billowy hoop skirts of square dancers, and that adoring fans everywhere were eager to conspire with ol' Hank in his time of need. A Pinkerton man was no challenge, as Oscar had learned in Indiana, where the detective posted outside the green room between shows was amazed to find Hank passed out from the miniatures, first floated in a pitcher of ice delivered to his hotel room and then stowed in his boots during his performance.

He slipped his handlers again before they had even checked in at a hotel in Des Moines, Iowa; when Oscar turned and couldn't find Hank after signing them in at the front desk, and asked a porter if he'd seen "the gentleman who was with me," he was directed to the bar, where he found Hank knocking down his second double bourbon on the rocks. When they were finally ensconced in room 505, with the detective outside guarding the door, Hank got to teasing Oscar: "I don't think I'll play tonight."

"What the hell are you talking about?"

"Naw, I just don't feel like it."

"You'd better, or you'll never play any other goddamn place."

"Anyways, you keep needling me about drinking."

Oscar picked up the phone and pretended to call Jim Denny at his home in Nashville. "I'm gonna tell Denny, 'I don't ever want this sonofabitch to ever play the Opry again.'"

"Aw, hell, I was just kidding."

"Here, then. I've got him on the line. *You* tell Jim Denny you were just kidding."

And he *didn't* play that night. As soon as Oscar had left the room, Hank dialed room 405 and said, "Look out your window." He had put a fifty-dollar bill in a laundry sack, with a scribbled note—saying he was just another traveler, too busy working, and needed two bottles of bourbon, keep the change—and lowered it with a "rope" made of sheets. Within half an hour he had hoisted the sack back up to his window and was having a party. When Oscar and the detective opened the door, they found Hank passed out drunk. Oscar tried to keep him away from the booze during the next stop, at the armory in Moline, Illinois, and a woman who was in the audience never forgot it: "Two men brought him out, one on each arm, his guitar around his neck, and stood him at the mike. He didn't say a word, not even howdy. He was like a zombie. He sang great for an hour and then the two men came and got him and took him away." Backstage afterward, she saw Hank propped up in a chair, "smelling like a brewery," so drunk that he "probably didn't know his name or where he was. But you talk about a performance. He never missed a note."

There was more of the same when Hank rolled into Baltimore to headline four shows a day for a solid week at the Hippodrome Theater. Even Don Helms, the most veteran of the Drifting Cowboys, had never seen him like this. ("Here I am in Baltimore," Hank would say at every show. "I ain't never been in Baltimore. If I come back, it'll be twice I been here.") Now Oscar had a genuine crisis on his hands. This was strike one against Hank, in case anybody in Nashville was keeping score, and Oscar knew they certainly were. He had to call in a mediocre country yodeler to fill Hank's place on the show, the first time this had become necessary on his watch, and out of desperation he had Audrey flown in from Nashville to see what she could do; which was, of course, to jump Hank like a chicken on a bug, telling everybody how personally embarrassed she was, and, since she was already there, to stick around and sing with Hank if he ever sobered up. His pattern for years had been to take three days to get smashed and three days to come out of it. Sure enough, by the time they reached D.C. Hank was up and running again. By invitation of Sen. John Sparkman of Alabama, he and Cowboy Copas set attendance records at the Victory Room in the Hotel Roosevelt—nine hundred came and five hundred were turned away—and when it was over, Hank, drunk again, having a good time, gave

Sparkman his wristwatch. The senator was still wearing it at
his death thirty-six years later.

As the year wound down, there was plenty to celebrate on
Franklin Road during the Christmas holidays of '49. It had
been Hank's breakout year—"Lovesick Blues," Opry mem-
bership, the tour of Europe, eight singles making the charts—
and now, having eclipsed his heroes Acuff and Tubb, he trailed
only Eddy Arnold in sales by a country performer. "Lovesick"
had sold two million records, "Wedding Bells" a million, and
Hank had earned $65,000 in MGM royalties alone. A public-
ity photo taken at the house showed a dozen healthy-looking
young Americans about to cash in on the postwar boom: Hank
and the four Drifting Cowboys, all wearing grins and their
stage costumes of boots and jaunty cowboy hats; their women,
a bit more subdued but smiling for the camera nevertheless,
guarding their young children. Out back the first of the ponies
Hank would buy for Lycrecia and Hank, Jr., was biding its
time in a corral, and the house was overflowing with the stuffed
animals and other gifts Daddy was wont to bring home from the
road in celebration of his fatherhood. The carport had already
been expanded in anticipation of the two new fishtail Cadillacs
on order: a green limo for Hank, and a yellow convertible for
Audrey, both of them sporting the latest power steering, power
brakes, and push-button windows. Hank's price for a show was
in the process of ballooning from $250 to $1,000-plus. There
seemed to be nowhere to go but up.

The possibility that Audrey would snap was always there,
though, and Hank had given her reason enough when he refused to let her sing with him during the gala in D.C. She had
left in a snit, returning alone to Nashville and the children,

and she was seething—again—when Hank got home, hung-
over and tired, pleased with himself; always himself, not them
as a husband-and-wife team. She had accompanied Hank on a
tour out west in the fall, and together they had run by Nudie
Cohen's Rodeo Tailors in Los Angeles, buying elaborate his-
and-hers costumes, but now her fringed cowgirl outfits hung
unused in the closet. It was always *Hank this* and *Hank that,*
but never Hank and Audrey. He already had all of the handlers and assistants he needed—Oscar Davis, Jim Denny,
Fred Rose, the Cowboys, even a banker—and, as they all
seemed to be making quite clear, he didn't need anybody to
help him sing. "[Audrey] was cocky, like Hank, and a tough
character," said Oscar Davis, remembering times when she,
without Hank, would enter a club: "She'd be dressed in dia-
monds and furs, and people were in awe, figuring she must be
somebody. When they found out she was Mrs. Hank Williams
they'd assume she could sing. 'Oh, just a little,' she'd say, and
when she did I wanted to hide. She was horrible, embarrassing." If nobody had confronted Audrey directly, they had certainly sent her messages that it was Hank, not Hank and
Audrey, who was being paid to perform. But she blamed Hank
for all of that.

As for Hank, whose only real experience with women was
with another of the same breed, mama Lillie, he could only try
to appease her with *things*: jewelry, clothes, cars, money for
the house. He was still continuing to plead her case to Fred
Rose, hoping to calm her down with another shot in the studio,
but Fred had already advised him that MGM had heard all it
could stand and maybe they could dump her off on somebody
else. Hank's hairline was receding; his back was killing him
from all that travel in a cramped car; his weight was sometimes

dipping into the 130s from the drinking and eating on the run; and it's quite likely that his libido was waning from the stress. Audrey had a good question—*What's in it for me?*—and her husband was damned if he had an answer. He had a monster to feed, a public that suddenly couldn't get enough, and maybe he could give them a piece of his soul.

Three Chords and the Truth

For the first time the word *genius* was being used to describe Hank, often with *tortured* attached, but that seemed overly simplistic. Tortured he was, mainly due to his lack of self-esteem and his bad luck with women and his dependence on alcohol to make things better, but "genius" connotes the inexplicable, and if you look deep enough you can find an explanation for just about anything. The Hank Williams who had evolved by 1950, scant months following his dramatic debut on the world scene, was the sum of his parts. He was a simple but sensitive man, poor and uneducated, just looking for love, and that's where he was coming from when he began expressing himself through his songs. He had no musical tricks up his sleeve, wouldn't know a simile or a metaphor unless somebody spelled it out for him, hardly knew a flat note from a sharp— indeed, some in the business would sneer, the boy couldn't even read music—but by now he was too rich to quit. Onstage and in the studio, he was doing what came naturally: desperately telling the story of his life, which kept getting worse. If he had a genius, it was for simplicity.

His partnership with Fred Rose was just that, arguably the most fortuitous collaboration in the history of American music. Rose took pains to downplay his role in the relationship ("Don't get the idea that I made the guy or wrote his songs for him," he said, insisting that Hank had "made himself"), but the more he denied his part in Hank's success the more his disclaimers were regarded as just further evidence of Fred's natural inclination toward modesty. True, he had been slow in the beginning to fully comprehend the sheer power of Hank's work and its appeal to the common man—Exhibit A would always be his utter misreading of "Lovesick Blues"—but as time went on he began to see that this could be a match made in heaven: the uneducated Hank would supply the raw material, and the technically proficient Fred would clean it up. Any writer in any discipline, from poetry to fiction to journalism, knows that Mitch Miller had it right when he said every good writer needs a good editor. Fred Rose had lived a hard life, himself, but he was either incapable or unwilling to write about it in such a direct manner; choosing, instead, to write catchy little ditties like " 'Deed I Do." Surely, it took his breath away when he saw a writer who could and would confront his hopes and fears and disappointments with such straightforward pain and clarity. Some of the songs were rough, needed work, and Fred figured that's where he came in if Hank would let him.

As it is in any relationship between a writer and an editor, they had their disagreements in the early days of working together. Fred learned early on not to force-feed Hank any more unsuitable material like "Rootie Tootie" and "Fly Trouble," stuff that was more Fred than Hank, preferring to sit back and look forward to those days when Hank would come in off the road and drop by the office (conveniently, a couple of miles from the house on Franklin Road), so they could go behind closed doors to tweak. *What you got?* Fred would say. *Folks kinda like this one,* Hank would tell him, producing a page from the spiral notebook he had filled with scribblings, everything from possible song titles to key lines to completed lyrics. Alone in Rose's office behind closed doors, or else at Fred's home studio, Hank would trot out a song's first draft, as it were, strumming and singing, closely watching Fred's eyes for a reaction. Fred might go to the piano to make a point about a chord change or a shift in rhythm or a better rhyme—*How about this?*—and so it would go for hours. Reluctantly at first, but with more confidence as their relationship deepened and the hits piled up, Hank became a willing partner. He would go along with Fred's changing the title from "I Lose Again" to "You Win Again," whatever "nuance" meant, as long as he'd let him continue speaking English as he and his fans in the countryside understood it: *pitcher* for picture, *keer* for care, *purr* for poor, and *pre-haps* for perhaps. Fred was beginning to get the hang of it, anyway; once, during a recording session, when one of the musicians asked if a take seemed "too country" he shot back, "It's *never* too country." (Well, maybe. Fred surely would have gone over the edge if he had heard Hank's pronunciation in a rendition of Acuff's "The Battle of Armageddon" during a show over KWKH in the pre-Rose days: *am-yer-gettin.*)

To be sure, there was some ammunition available for the songwriters who argued that Fred played a much larger part in the making of Hank's music than he publicly admitted, but it was scant and had more to do with arrangements than with lyrics. "Move It on Over" had a touch that was purely Fred Rose, with his Tin Pan Alley orientation—a recurring answer from the band members, who would chant "move it on over" every time Hank sang the title line—a technique used by the big dance bands, most notably Glenn Miller in his version of "Pennsylvania 6-5000." In one of Hank's last recordings, "I

Won't Be Home No More," the lyrics were decidedly Hank, but the sassy swing rhythm is just as surely attributable to Rose. The lyrics and the tom-tom drumbeat in "Kaw-Liga" (credited as "Words by Fred Rose, Music by Hank Williams") were mostly Hank's creations, as is well documented in accounts of his last days on earth, but Fred fine-tuned the title and came up with the "envelope" for the story (a shy cigar-store Indian misses the Indian maiden "down by the antique store" who has been sold away) and recommended changing chords between the opening and the driving chorus. Except for trying to keep Hank away from mentions of booze, and for finding a better word here or there, that was about it. What really seemed to discombobulate Hank's disbelievers was the poeticism of "I'm So Lonesome I Could Cry." They simply could not believe that this barely literate hillbilly could write lines like that—of lonesome whippoorwills, purple skies, weeping robins, midnight trains whining low, a moon going behind a cloud to hide its face and cry—forgetting that young Hiram Williams had spent a lonesome childhood in the dark forests of Alabama with those as his only companions. The city boy, Fred Rose, probably cried like everybody else when he first heard it.

Where Fred truly excelled, as a producer, was in the arrangement of a piece of music—finding the right meter, the proper key, the instrumentation, the perfect sound to complement the lyrics—and it hadn't taken long at all for him to discover the secret to a Hank Williams song: the simpler the better. One of the Willis brothers had played accordion during Hank's first recording session, but that was dropped. During subsequent sessions, the same fate befell mandolins, organs, pianos, and drums. All were deemed out of character with Hank's minimalist imagery. More than one sideman had been excoriated for trying to get too fancy—"A lot of pickers has ed-ucated themselves right out of a job," Hank once warned one of them—and "vanilla" became the byword onstage and in the studio. Fred tried to put himself in the seat of a listener, whether in the cheap seats of a large auditorium or on a bar stool in a noisy juke joint or in the cab of a truck with wind whistling and gears grinding, and he knew that the sweet nu-ances of, say, a string quartet would be utterly lost. He wanted a sound that could be heard above all of that. Thus, he had boiled the instrumentation down to a thumping bass fiddle and the countering "crack" of a guitar to set the basic beat, a rhythm guitar to carry the key, an electric guitar to rhyme with the melody, a fiddle played the old-fashioned way (two strings in harmony, not one, which made it too tempting to go off on riffs), and an echoing steel guitar played in the highest ranges so it could be heard above any outside noises. Only the fiddle and the steel would take turns on solos, merely as brief respites before the spotlight went back to Hank resuming his confessional tales. Years later, a highly regarded songwriter named Harlan Howard would famously coin a phrase to define country music in general but in fact describe the entire Hank Williams oeuvre: "three chords and the truth."

When he turned the calendar to bring on a new year, 1950, Hank for the first time was feeling the pressure to come up with a hit record. "Bucket" and some others had done well enough, kept him on the charts and in the money, but he needed another blockbuster like "Lovesick Blues." He and Fred were moving ever closer to their own understanding of what a Hank Williams song was all about—the haunting sound and the aching intensity of the lyrics to express the simple needs of a man in pain—and by now Hank himself had coldly calculated how to go for the jugular. Methodically, word by word and line by line, he had been scribbling away on a song that contained all of the buzzwords and phrases: *lonesome, cold as ice, pay the price, wanted to die,* a woman who *couldn't be true* and *made me blue,* those *long gone but not forgotten blues.* Just as the title of "I Saw the Light" had come from a chance remark, so did he make a discovery that would kick-start the tune he would entitle "Long Gone Lonesome Blues." On a fishing excursion to one of the lakes north of Nashville, with Hank's mind somewhere else, his impatient partner had said, "You come here to fish or watch the fish swim by?" Hank said, "That's it, that's the first line," and he couldn't wait to get back home and write it down. Written to order, it had everything, including room for the heartbreaking blue yodels that had distinguished "Lovesick."

They gathered on a January afternoon at Castle Studio in the Tulane Hotel, where Hank would cut all of the remaining records in his career, and this would mark the first time the core of the Drifting Cowboys—Don Helms and Jerry Rivers—had backed him in a studio. Beginning with "Long Gone Lonesome Blues," all four of the tunes on the docket for that day's work were classic lamentations written by Hank. They had barely unpacked their instruments and begun to warm up when Fred left the booth and sidled over to Helms. "Don't ever go below this mark," he said, laying his finger on a fret: his way of signaling that the steel guitar on a Hank Williams record was to be played in the highest range, to complement Hank's twang and to be heard over extant noise. "You want to make it cry, and we want to be sure it can be heard on a jukebox." Rose had done his research, knew that three-fifths of Hank's record sales were to jukebox operators. There might be some sixteen million people out there who owned home phonographs now, but each of them bought an average of only ten records a year; there were just 400,000 jukeboxes, on the other hand, and they had ravenous appetites—each of the nation's 5,500 jukebox "ops" were buying 150 records every *week*. Helms certainly understood without being told. Hell, he had practically *invented* the way Hank's steel should sound, as though he had been born to play for Hank Williams and nobody else. That understood, the day's work began. Helms opened cold with the chorus, and in stepped Hank: "I went down to the river to watch the fish swim by. . . ." They cut four sides that day, including "Why Don't You Love Me (Like You Used to Do)," another of Hank's most-remembered hits, and went home to rest.

For some time, Hank had been badgering Fred to let him record some "recitations," the moralistic little homilies that he had performed from time to time on his radio shows. With his childhood memories of the church, and his adult feelings of whiskey-driven guilt, through these he saw a way toward atonement. It was sappy stuff, for the most part: truly bad poems dealing with sin and salvation and country gumption and what all, begging for a church organ in the background. They were a long way from the songs that were making Hank famous, and Fred was adamantly opposed, out of deference to the jukebox operators if nothing else. Virtually all of the operators serviced honky-tonks, Hank biographer Colin Escott points out, "and the last thing they needed was for someone to punch up a Hank Williams record and get a sermon." Bending to Hank's pressure, Fred finally agreed but with a major request: that they not be recorded under Hank's name. They finally settled on a nom de plume—"Luke the Drifter"—so the jukebox people wouldn't be led astray. On that day following the cuts of "Long Gone Lonesome" and "Why Don't You Love Me," two sure smash hits that were classic Hank tunes, they put down four weepy recitations dealing with a poor black kid's funeral, an old farmer's optimism in the face of ruin, something called "Too Many Parties and Too Many Pals," and even a piece of doggerel written by the Pittsburgh Pirates' baseball announcer. The services of Jerry Rivers on the fiddle weren't needed on these; only Hank's voice, a bass fiddle and an organ, and Helms's steel. When they had finished the first of them, "The Funeral," both Hank and Helms were seen standing in the studio with tears streaming down their faces. To their credit, nobody involved in the recitations ever denied the true identity of Luke the Drifter—not that there was any doubt—and that particular genre had a separate life of its own, intended for what Hank dismissed as the "take-home trade." No harm was done; like the British literary novelist Graham Greene, who kissed off his lighter works as "entertainments," Hank had gotten it out of his system. Luke the Drifter was the flip side of Hank's split personality: the penitent, moralizing about the bad things the other Hank had done.

Sure enough, "Long Gone Lonesome Blues" did the trick, replacing "Chattanoogie Shoe Shine Boy" at the top of the *Billboard* country chart upon its release in the spring and staying at No. 1 for eight weeks. It had sold 150,000 copies by August ("The Funeral," by comparison, had sold only 6,600), to be replaced at the top by "Why Don't You Love Me," meaning that the work from that January session had more or less guaranteed Hank a handsome income for the year. Now all he had to do was hit the road and earn it, which was easier said than done. The real money in those days came from personal appearances, not from records or songwriting royalties or sales of sheet music and publicity photos. His income in 1950 would top out at $92,500, the great bulk of it coming from road shows, where he might pick up $2,000 for headlining at a big auditorium one night and settle for $250 to work a roadhouse the next. It's inaccurate to say that now he had "only" to go on the road, because with every passing mile the road was becoming a killer. It seemed only a matter of time before Hank would have to look into surgery to address his back problems, and the long automobile trips (even if it was in a roomier Cadillac) weren't helping. Trouble seemed to find him out there: young women throwing themselves at him, good old boys insisting on buying him a drink, the repetition driving him to get drunk soon enough, all of that ultimately leading to his falling apart in the midst of a tour and being shipped back home to face Audrey. Sometimes she might be there when he dragged in, unannounced, and sometimes she might not: *The news is out all over town / That you've been seen a-runnin' 'round.* . . . It worked both ways. Each of the two, certain that the other was having an affair, would launch one in retaliation.

What to do about Audrey, as long as she insisted on sharing the bill with her husband, the most valuable commodity in country music? The bigger Hank got, the more problematical she became. Whatever went on behind closed doors on Franklin Road, and it surely wasn't pleasant, the powers-that-were wanted nothing to do with her when it came to making music because she was awful at it. But who was going to tell her?

Fred Rose and MGM and Oscar Davis and the Opry and WSM had left every hint imaginable—deadening her microphone, leaving her name off marquees, dropping her from radio shows, refusing to record her on duets, leaving it up to Hank whether she would accompany him on the stage of the Ryman— but still she wouldn't go away. Both she and Hank knew that he owed her a big debt, that it was her burning drive that had gotten him to Nashville in the first place, and in her eyes only Hank could help her fulfill her dreams. The poor man was stuck right in the middle.

Whether it was Hank's clever answer to the quandary is open to conjecture, but in the spring of '50 there came an opportunity to force the issue. After some horse-trading that ensued when Decca failed to wrest Hank from MGM, Audrey suddenly came up with her own recording contract. She would go into a studio and make records to her heart's content—*Sing it, babe!*—and maybe she would get it out of her system, once and for all. She would start with Hank's "Honky Tonkin'" and do a Hadacol tune called "What Put the Pep in Grandpa," cutting a half dozen sides in all during a three-hour session. Hank was there, of course, and so were the Drifting Cowboys, getting union scale and a front-row seat for the showdown. *Haddy- call! Haddy-call! Haddy-call!* Helms and Rivers and the rest yelped in answer to Audrey's refrain during "Pep in Grandpa," surely making the folks from Hadacol cringe every time they heard it. Not surprisingly, the records bombed at the box office and with the critics when they were released in the fall, as did a couple of the Hank-and-Audrey gospel duets that MGM had been withholding for a couple of years. Did that cool her off? Of course not; it was, as usual, somebody else's fault.

Audrey's carping only intensified after that, her way of getting even for a career that now, obviously, would never happen. She adjusted her sights and aimed them full-time on her husband. "Just don't tell Ordrey," Hank was always reminding the band whenever he had gotten drunk or had a romantic escapade with a female fan or otherwise screwed up on the road, just as he once had pleaded that nobody tell his mother. He was expecting an ass-kicking when he got home, anyway, guilty or not, and usually he fell off the wagon as a tour was ending. The work was over, the money was in his pocket, and Audrey was waiting, so he might as well get drunk. There was a sanitarium in Madison, a town north of Nashville, near Don Helms's house in Hendersonville, and it became routine for Helms to drop him off there without even bothering to call Audrey in advance. "We all had families by then, so nobody could take him home." Out back of the place was a series of little stone cottages, each with barred windows and a cot and a toilet, and every time Hank saw them looming, as he awakened from his drunken stupor, he would bolt upright in the limo: "Oh, no, not the hut! Not again!" Once admitted, he slept, gobbled the food slipped to him, took the candy and comic books Helms brought him, and after a couple of days he would be ready to go again. "He'd say, 'Reckon when they're gonna let us out?' I'd say, '*We* ain't in, hoss,'" said Helms.

The fact is, practicing moderation was a concept totally foreign to Hank. He wanted everything now, not later, and he scooped it up in large doses. He couldn't just go fishing: that required a dozen poles, enough bait to feed every fish in the lake, snacks and beer to last a couple of days, and if he anchored over a school of bream or crappie he might stay until midnight. He went hunting armed to the teeth, as though gone to war. One pony for Bocephus and Lycrecia wasn't enough;

soon he had collected a herd. Talk of guns led him to seek the help of local cops on the road so he could buy up virtual arsenals of antique pistols and blunderbusses. If he chanced upon a carnival while on tour and started winning stuffed animals to take home to the kids, the Cowboys wondered how they were going to find room for themselves and their instruments in the car. He couldn't have just one Cadillac, one woman, one aspirin, or just one drink.

Don Helms became the expert on Hank and his drinking: "Nobody could have had that kind of career, drunk. He was sober ninety-eight percent of the time, but when he started drinking it was over. He wouldn't cause us any trouble. We'd just ignore him. The thing is, he couldn't just have a drink. A couple, and he was drunk. Everything he did, in fact, was bad for him: the drinking, the smoking, not eating. He wasn't a pill-head or a junkie, but if he read on a label where it said to take one pill every four hours he'd take four pills every hour, figuring that'd work four times faster. The only thing he ever did about pills was overuse 'em. I never saw Hank drunk in the studio, and they usually managed to get him off the stage before he'd get into trouble." Helms and Hank took up hunting and bowling together, but Hank's favorite escape was to get in a boat and fish all day on the lakes north of the city. Audrey could find him anywhere, it seemed. Jerry Rivers remembered a day when they were out on Kentucky Lake, boys' day off, and were startled to see a seaplane landing on the water; soon, here came Audrey in a motorboat, all excited, telling Hank there was a phone call he just had to return, and he obediently followed her home.

She never backed off; indeed, she turned up the heat after seeing her own hopes for celebrity crumble. "I don't care what

you do with the son of a bitch, just don't bring him out here,"
she would tell Helms or whoever called ahead to say they were
bringing Hank home and he was drunk. Once she did call
back, to ask where her money was, and got her comeuppance
from the musician in charge of Hank on that particular excursion: "Lady, as far as I'm concerned you ain't got no damned
money. I gave *Hank's* money to Jim Denny." Only two weeks
after her recording session for Decca, in fact, she locked the
doors on him and he was forced to check into the Tulane Hotel,
where he fell asleep with a cigarette in his hand, setting fire to
the room, was arrested, and paid a fifteen-dollar fine. Their relationship was heading downhill fast, and in the most public of
ways. The two daily newspapers in Nashville were fairly benign in those days, leaving the goings-on in the music business
to take care of itself, but word-of-mouth was a factor. Members
of the inbred Opry cast had learned to hold their breath when
Audrey came through the stage-door entrance to the Ryman on
a Saturday night with Hank, all suited up in her cowgirl outfit,
and bets were made on whether he would ignore her or invite
"Miss Ordrey" to join him to sing onstage. The Nashville police certainly didn't have to ask directions anymore to 4916
Franklin Road. And by now the record-buying public was beginning to connect the dots and figure out the "inspiration," if
that was the word, for Hank's torrent of hits dealing with love
gone wrong.

When Hank threw a drunk, it could take bizarre turns. For
whatever reasons, come that summer he had decided to dump
Oscar Davis as his manager—Oscar wouldn't get off his case
about the booze, or else Hank simply didn't like cutting someone in on his take—so he had made a deal for himself to star at
one of the biggest annual events on the country music circuit:

the July Fourth Watermelon Festival at a little outpost called DeLeon, smack in the middle of Texas. Many of the big stars were going to be there, none bigger than Hank, and all he had to do to earn his $3,000 guarantee was show up at ten o'clock in the morning and sing. Ten o'clock came, and noon, and there was still no Hank. The crowd of farmers and their families had swelled to eleven thousand people, and they were growing mutinous under the searing sun when Hank's limo came slithering to a stop around two in the afternoon. Their excitement rose, and just as quickly plummeted. Hank was in there, but he wouldn't get out. The promoter, who happened to be the town's mayor, walked over to the limo to see what the problem was and found that Hank was royally drunk. A man identifying himself as his "personal manager" said Hank was too "sick" to go on. The chief of police was summoned. The "manager" was handcuffed to the steering wheel and Hank was pulled out of the car and dragged to the stage where two men held him up for inspection. "Hank Williams's manager says he's too sick to perform," the mayor said, "but if you were standing as close to him as I am you'd know what he's sick from." Hank nearly fell to his knees when the men let him go, and he had to stagger back to the limo under a rain of boos. The Opry rushed in Hank Snow to take his place the next night at the auditorium in Dallas, and Hank was flown back to Nashville a step ahead of another booker ready to skin his hide: Jack Ruby—*that* Jack Ruby—a small-time mobster whose nightclub Hank had failed to grace during the same trip.

For Hank Williams, the recording star, these interludes were just that: little bumps in the road, things that came up, situations soon forgotten. Ever since his first recording session in

1946, when he curtly rejected the very idea of having so much
as a beer beforehand, he had treated the studio as his church,
his laboratory, his one true friend. This was where everything
started. Without the records, there would be nothing—no
Opry, no concerts, no clamoring crowds, no royalties, no
career—and he knew it. Whatever might be happening in his
personal life, he closed it behind him when he walked into the
studio. Of the legions of Drunk Hank Stories that have
amassed in his wake, not one of them takes place anywhere
near a recording session. The studio was sacrosanct. There,
within those cushioned walls, stone-cold sober, making music
with his friends, you found the truest measure of Hank
Williams. There, nothing mattered but the songs. There is
where he took everything he knew—the pain, the regrets, the
joys, the sorrows—and channeled it all into a microphone, to
be recorded for posterity. Everything else, as far as he was
concerned, was beside the point. *Know me, know my music.*
How he got there was one thing, prurient gossip for the masses.
What he put in the groove was everything.

By now, with his personal life beginning to unravel, he
seemed to be making no pretensions about what mattered
most. He had produced some "entertainments," for lack of a
better word—"Pan American" and "My Bucket's Got a Hole
in It" and "I'm a Long Gone Daddy"—but as he was nearing
the end of his second year on the national stage he began going
straight to the heart of the matter. What was expected from
Hank Williams was a song about heartache, the gut-felt emotions of a man in a desperate search for love, and he was glad
to oblige. The jukeboxes and the airwaves were beginning to
fill with them, their titles being fair warning: "Long Gone
Lonesome Blues," "Why Don't You Love Me," "Nobody's

Lonesome for Me," "Moanin' the Blues," "Why Should We Try Anymore," and "Cold, Cold Heart." The stuff was pure journalism, set to music, a journal of his life with Audrey. From now until his last recording session, when he cut "Your Cheatin' Heart" with little more than three months left to live, that was the primary drive in his life.

Sobered up from the debacle in Texas, he had gone back to work as though nothing had happened—more touring, another recording session, still more touring—but in September of '50 here came another chapter in the marriage. Unbeknownst to Hank, Audrey had gotten pregnant. Whether the father was her husband or one of her growing number of suitors will never be known. But she didn't tell anybody about it, choosing instead to abort the fetus in an operation at home. An infection had set in, sending her to the hospital, and that's where Hank was told he could find her when he dragged in off the road to find her gone. He rounded up some flowers and jewelry and hustled off to the hospital to see her, but when he tried to kiss her and present the peace offerings she threw them in his face: "You sorry son of a bitch! It was you that caused me to suffer this." When he skulked home, he remarked to the housekeeper, "That woman's got a cold, cold heart." It sounded like a song to Hank, when he got to thinking about it, and within three months he was in the Castle Studio recording the one that would throw him into an entirely new orbit.

Lonely at the Top

The song he wrote about this latest unpleasantness from Audrey was called "Cold, Cold Heart," and the lyrics read like another page torn from Hank's diary. Every time a man tries to show his love that "you're my every dream" it backfires on him; she suspects that whatever he does is "just some evil scheme"; he can't win for losing. Don Helms and Jerry Rivers were backing Hank in the studio on that night four days before Christmas (along with a new young guitarist in town by the name of Chet Atkins), and they felt a tingle that was becoming all too familiar, the feel of working on a record that was going to be around for a long time. The boss was at it again with some more of the Audrey stuff, something they knew more about than they cared to discuss. When Hank closed it out with his woeful lament—"How can I free your doubtful mind and melt your cold, cold heart"—they knew he had another winner. They just didn't know exactly how big this one would become.

For too long, country music had been regarded as the bastard child of American musical forms, unsophisticated wailings from the outback, primitive utterings best left to historians and sociologists, artifacts from some lost civilization to be studied by archaeologists. Even *Billboard*, the weekly magazine of record for commercial American music, had been slow in its recognition, first calling it "hillbilly" music, then "folk," and only now "country." The power of the music's simplicity and its consequent appeal to the common folk was lost on Tin Pan Alley, the brotherhood of tunesmiths in New York City and Chicago, musical sophisticates busy churning out mindless little ditties like "Mairzy Doats," which may have been the height of their folly: "mares eat oats and does eat oats . . ." On the occasions when big-name pop singers like Bing Crosby and Frank Sinatra deigned to play around with country material, as Crosby did in '43 with "Pistol Packin' Mama," it was done with snickering condescension. They were slumming. It was country, they were telling their fans, but they'd get over it.

Fred Rose knew better, and it was *because* he had come out of Tin Pan Alley. Nobody had ever written lyrics like Hank and he knew it. This was what had led him to hire Mitch Miller, the goateed producer of pop music at Columbia Records, to see about expanding Hank's audience beyond the country charts. (Miller had met Hank once and found him to be "shy. The only times he was at ease was when he was performing or writing.") Both Rose and Miller knew there was a universality in Hank's lyrics that spoke as clearly to a hardware salesman in Georgia as to a stockbroker on Wall Street—"In anger unkind words are said that make the teardrops start"—and so it was that Miller presented Hank's demo of the new song to a promising young pop crooner named Tony Bennett, still looking for his first hit record. "Oh, no, don't make me do cowboy songs," Bennett said when he first heard the fiddle and the steel guitar and Hank's backwoods pronunciations. "The words, Tony," Miller told him, "listen to the words." Miller put a full-blown philharmonic orchestra behind Bennett, and when his gussied-up version of "Cold, Cold Heart" came out it rocketed to the top of the pop charts. Other cover versions of Hank's tunes began cropping up soon, by artists as varied as Louis Armstrong, Perry Como, and Dinah Washington, and a new day was born. Now all of the major labels were scrambling to find material that was basically country—Patti Page's "Tennessee Waltz" was among them—and it was the team of Williams/Rose/Miller that had made it so. The pop music crowd held to its patronizing mode, a *Billboard* story being headlined "There's Gold in Them Thar Hillbilly Tunes," and a trade-magazine ad reading "Popcorn! A Top Corn Tune Gone Pop." Personally, Hank didn't much care for Bennett's slick version of his "Cold, Cold Heart"—what he was hearing on the jukeboxes being a far cry from what he had felt that day at the hospital when Audrey threw his get-well gifts back in his face—but all of a sudden his songwriting royalties began doubling with the additional exposure.

After less than two years in Nashville, he had transcended the narrow confines of country music. Tony Bennett was only the first noncountry performer to capitalize on the broad appeal of songs written by Hank Williams. Fifty years after Hank's death, an astonishing array of musicians from nearly every possible genre had recorded his work—such disparate singers and instrumentalists as the Bee Gees, James Brown, Nat King Cole, the Grateful Dead, Isaac Hayes, Lou Rawls, Elvis Presley, Guy Lombardo, Frankie Laine, even Lawrence Welk—a remarkable legacy for a man from nowhere, an uneducated country boy from the wilds of south Alabama, someone who lived on the dark side of the musical establishment. Just as Ernest Hemingway didn't believe in similes (instead of writing that something is "like" something else, why not say *precisely* what it is?), Hank, who probably had never even heard of Hemingway, innately dealt with the rawest emotions in the simplest language. Mitch Miller was among those who ranked him with another natural American icon, Stephen Foster: "He had a way of reaching your guts and your head at the same time. No matter who you were, a country person or a sophisticate, the language hit home. Nobody I know could use basic English so effectively. Every song socks you in the gut." Hank himself was damned if he could explain it the few times he was asked. "You got to have smelled a lot of mule manure before you can sing like a hillbilly," he once said, illuminating nothing except his playful predilection to play the *aw-shucks* game with the few reporters who came around.

With all of this money and celebrity going for him, he was finally gaining confidence in himself. Gone was the backwoods naïf content to stay close to home in somnolent Montgomery rather than go for the brass ring in Nashville, and in his place was a genuine superstar not above letting everybody know it. From the very beginning, when he arrived at the Opry to find "Candy Kisses" blocking his "Lovesick Blues" from the top of the country charts, he made fun of George Morgan's "silly" lyrics. Whether on tour with other Opry stars or backstage at the Ryman, he was beginning to get on the nerves of his fellow singers with a routine that got old in a hurry: he would run a new tune by them, get a favorable response, and then say it was "too damned good for you," that he would record it himself. He took a dismissive view about how pop musicians were suddenly discovering his country songs: "These pop bands will only play our hillbilly songs when they can't eat any other

way." He even called Tony Bennett to needle him good-
naturedly when "Cold, Cold Heart" made it big in the pop
charts ("Hey, Tony, how come you ruined my song?"). Whenever he and the band stopped for a bite to eat in a diner, his
first move was to pump nickels into the jukebox to play every
Hank Williams song it had, taking particular pleasure now in
punching the versions recorded by pop singers. Whether
drunk or sober, he even began taking it out on any fan or artist
who failed to genuflect properly: "How much money did *you*
make today? When you've made a thousand dollars, then we
can talk." One night when he stumbled onstage in Lafayette,
Louisiana, too drunk to perform, he waited until the catcalls
had subsided before speaking into the microphone: "I bet y'all
drove a long way to see ol' Hank, didn't you?" It was true and
the crowd cheered. "Well, now you've seen him," he said, laying his guitar on the floor, turning on his heels, and stalking
off, leaving another mess for somebody else to clean up.

On the way to grossing some $150,000 in 1951, Hank began
joining Audrey in spending money before he had it, to the extent that a personal manager he had hired swore that Hank often couldn't cover a ten-dollar check. Their idea of a savings
account was discovering some misplaced bills left in a coat
pocket or coins spilled between the cushions of a sofa. They
had both grown up in rural poverty, during the Depression, and
now it seemed they were in competition to see who could
spend the most the fastest. Together, they would set the standard for a caricature that would heap ridicule upon Nashville
for many generations to come: country musicians with more
money than taste, surrounding themselves with things, trying
to buy their way into "acceptable" society with fleets of new

cars, gaudy palaces, ornate swimming pools, and other play-
things of the nouveau riche. Audrey had set the pace from the
beginning of their life in Nashville, with her furs and her jewelry and her never-ending expansion of the house on Franklin
Road—it now contained seven bedrooms, six and a half bath-
rooms, a chandeliered ballroom, a garage expanded to include
an upstairs "mother-in-law" apartment (no mothers-in-law invited, though, God forbid)—and Hank had begun to pitch in
with a well-appointed bar, of all things, a fully equipped music
room, and more Cadillacs: a coupe for him, a convertible for
Audrey, and the spacious touring limousine. He would come in
off the road with more trinkets and stuffed animals for Hank,
Jr., and Lycrecia, and matched sets of expensive collectors'
pistols for himself, only to find that Audrey had been busy
keeping up: more tasteless furniture, additions to her
wardrobe, and new closets to put the stuff in.

Figuring every cowboy ought to have a farm, Hank went out
and bought one—a five-hundred-acre spread southward toward the little town of Franklin—writing a check for $15,000
toward the $60,000 purchase price. There was a dilapidated
antebellum farmhouse on the land, and his long-range plans
included refurbishing the house and making it their primary
residence. He bought a Tennessee walking horse, moved the
kids' ponies from Franklin Road, added some white-faced cattle, had fences built, and hired a manager to look after the
stock. It was his dream to be a gentleman rancher, going back
to his days of watching cowboy-and-Indians "pitcher shows"
as a kid in south Alabama, but nothing much came of it. His
concert schedule kept him on the road most of the time; his
bad back precluded his spending much time astride a horse;
and Audrey was running *from* farm life, not toward it, meaning

she visited the place only for photo ops or to bring the kids when they wanted to ride. Hank wound up spending a lot of time out there alone, drinking and thinking and firing his guns. If nothing else, he and his business manager figured, the expenses of buying and running the place would give him a tax write-off.

Well, then, how about a country store downtown? Again trying to guess what might finally make Audrey happy, he envisioned a place—Hank and Audrey's Corral—stocked with western clothing, records, songbooks, signed photographs, Hank and Audrey dolls, picture postcards, the kinds of doodads that visitors to the Opry would surely want to buy. He had envied Ernest Tubb's Record Shop, around the corner from the Ryman, and this was his response. Renting a space nearby on Commerce Street, he stocked it with $7,000 worth of inventory, had it tackied up in faux log-cabin décor (wagon wheels, board-and-batten walls, oil lamps, lots of fake buckskin), and had great hopes for the endeavor during the grand opening on a summer's Saturday. Hank and Audrey were there in their western finery, performing with the Drifting Cowboys, as was Roy Acuff. The plan was to broadcast live shows over WSM from the Corral every Saturday afternoon, to complement the post-Opry show from Tubb's Record Shop, but crowds got so large that the show had to be moved to the WSM studios. As it turned out, people were more interested in hearing Hank sing up close and for free than in buying his boots and hats and shirts. In short order, the business became a drag; Hank had to go in on weekend mornings to write checks, and the only times Audrey came around was to tap the till for spare cash on the first leg of a shopping spree. It became a hangout for footloose musicians, eager to see Hank and pitch their songs, and before long he was hiring a full-time manager for the store and walking away from it. It had turned out to be more trouble than it was worth.

It's not that he was bored; far from it. In spite of the squabbling with Audrey and his drinking disasters and back problems, Hank filled two hundred dates all over the country that year. Now and then he would settle in one city for a few days, headlining a spectacular package show, but for the most part he was out there on the road playing one-nighters from town to town. The two-hour Hank Williams road show had a familiar beginning, middle, and end: a warm-up by the Drifting Cowboys, including a cornball routine by the bass-playing comedian; Hank being brought on for forty-five minutes; an intermission, during which the band members went into the crowd to hawk songbooks and photographs; Hank coming back onstage to close out the show. He had been at this long enough to know how to pace an evening's entertainment: a slow weeper here, some country patter there, something to get 'em jumping, a little introspection from Luke the Drifter, then a show-stopping closer. He was a handsome scoundrel—*dangerous*—and the women, especially, greeted him with screams and wild applause when he sauntered out onto the stage in his double-breasted western-cut outfit from Nudie's of Hollywood, the Stetson and the high-heeled boots making him loom taller than his lanky six-one. The lessons he had learned from Tee-Tot Payne as a kid pitching songs on the sidewalks of Georgiana and Greenville were serving him well. "Here's one we been eatin' off for a while," he would drawl before announcing "Hey, Good Lookin'" or "Cold, Cold Heart," hunkering over the microphone, strumming the guitar, tapping his feet, swaying to the sounds of Don Helms's crying steel on the introduction, seeming to pick out one face in the crowd with his piercing brown eyes before he took off running. He had a way of connecting with an audience that made each song sound like a private serenade, something he had been saving for just this crowd, on this night only, *because y'all been so good to me.* Indeed, when he was in the very midst of crafting "Jambalaya," he did something Helms had never seen before: previewed a work-in-progress. They were playing an auditorium in southern Louisiana, where the Cajuns were wild about Hank, and he knew they were going to love this one: "He told 'em he was still working on this song and he'd like to know what they thought. So he started it—'Goodbye Joe, me gotta go, me oh my oh; Me gotta go pole the pirogue down the bayou'—and they went crazy. He sang all he had at that point and then stopped. Said he'd sing the rest of it next time back, when he'd finished it." And always, there was the close: "If the good Lord's willin' and the creek don't rise, we'll see you next time."

He had enough money now that he could afford to charter a plane if there was a long jump to the next date, or if he had to rush back to fill his obligations to the Opry on a Saturday night, the band pushing ahead with the equipment in the Cadillac limo. (The air taxi for the stars in those days belonged to Minnie Pearl's wealthy husband, Henry Cannon, who owned a spiffy single-engine Beechcraft Bonanza.) For the most part, though, Hank and the Cowboys stayed to sign autographs, pose for snapshots, sell some more records and songbooks, and collect the cash—he had stopped taking checks after being burned once too often—before loading up the car and driving on to the next stop, sometimes eight hours down a two-lane asphalt highway that cut right through the middle of every city or

town along the way. They would sleep, shower, and eat whenever they could get around to it. For example, they began one
two-week stretch in the spring of '51 on Friday, March 23, with
a recording session in Nashville, working the Opry on Saturday night, then hitting the road: Sunday, concert in Evansville,
Indiana; Monday, traveling through Indiana and Illinois; Tuesday, concert in a gymnasium in Decatur, Illinois; Wednesday,
playing the Community Center in Centralia, Illinois; Thursday,
working the Arena Theatre in Paducah, Kentucky; Friday, the
high school auditorium in Mount Vernon, Illinois; Saturday,
the Opry; Sunday, matinee and evening performances in Little
Rock, Arkansas; Monday, appearing in Monroe, Louisiana;
Tuesday, at the high school auditorium in Baton Rouge,
Louisiana; Wednesday, a return to Municipal Auditorium in
Shreveport, the scene of Hank's triumphs during his days on
the Louisiana Hayride; Thursday, outdoors in the ballpark in
Corpus Christi, Texas; Friday, Municipal Auditorium in New
Orleans; Saturday, back to the Opry and home. The advent of
the cushy touring bus was a few years away, and the road was
literally a killer. But they were young and eager and relatively
healthy, doing exactly what they wanted to do, and when things
were going well with Hank—no booze, no fights, no cooling
heels in the parking lot of a motel while Hank bedded a girl
inside—it was good enough for men who otherwise might have
been spending their lives at hard labor in fields or factories.
("Quit?" said Don Helms. "Hell, I was in show business.")
One time they piled into the limo at seven on a Sunday morning, for an afternoon matinee in Birmingham, a five-hour drive
in those days, and when they arrived Hank had written "Hey,
Good Lookin'" from start to finish.

Between road shows, they managed to work in the bread-

and-butter recording sessions, the ones that would seal Hank's
true legacy. Like a baseball player who knows he'll be remembered not for his performances in spring training or during the
dog days of a waning summer but in the high-intensity play-
offs and World Series, Hank was fully wired when he walked
into the studio: stone-cold sober, all business, thoroughly con-
centrated, knowing this was for all time. Six times he went into
Castle Studio that year, and he came out of it with an astonishing number of recordings that would shame anybody who had
ever sung a country song. To name only the truly great ones he
recorded that year, there were "I Can't Help It (If I'm Still in
Love with You)," "Hey, Good Lookin'," "(I Heard That) Lonesome Whistle," "Crazy Heart," "Baby, We're Really in Love,"
"Half as Much," and "Honky Tonk Blues." Except for Bennett's rendition of "Cold, Cold Heart," none of the crossover
versions topped Hank's original recordings in sales and criti-
cal acclaim, and they certainly aren't remembered half a century later, because they simply lacked the earnest emotional
tug, the credibility, the *oomph*, delivered by Hank himself.
Now Mitch Miller had his hands full, deciding which of the
pop singers he should choose from all of those clamoring to
cover Hank's latest.

Two years after his debut on the Opry, Hank was the acknowledged king of country music. All of the others had re-
ceded in his wake, some of them his heroes before he got there.
Bob Wills and the Texas Playboys had a fervent regional following, mainly in the dance halls of Oklahoma and Texas, but
they were oddities east of the Mississippi. Ernest Tubb was an
Opry regular, beloved in Texas, but he seemed to have topped
out as a big man on the jukebox-and-roadhouse scene. Eddy
Arnold was still selling more records than anybody based in

Nashville, but he was more pop than country with his sweet uptown orchestrations like "Anytime (You're Feeling Lonely)" and "I'm Sending You a Big Bouquet of Roses." Roy Acuff had lost his recording contract and seemed content to anchor the Opry every weekend, singing "Wabash Cannonball," reminding his aging fans of the music's Appalachian roots. Much the same could be said of the revered Carter Family. New arrivals would come and go—George Morgan, Carl Smith, Lefty Frizzell, Louisiana governor Jimmie Davis ("You Are My Sunshine"), even the cowboy movie star Tex Ritter—but none had the staying power to threaten Hank's domination. In his personal life and his demeanor, along with his natural talent, Hank had set the mold for the quintessential "hillbilly" singer: rawboned, emotional, tortured, unmanageable. *Sing your heart out, country boy!* He was to country music what Frank Sinatra was to pop, and what Elvis Presley would soon become to the teenagers all over the world. He was the Man. And he scared the hell out of the cautious Protestant guardians of the Grand Ole Opry's family image.

Almost as a respite from all of this, Hank was hailed as a local-boy-made-good when the Montgomery Jaycees staged a Hank Williams Homecoming in his adopted hometown on a Saturday in mid-July. He had come a long, long way since the wartime years when he nearly gave up the business out of despair— living in his mother's boardinghouse, playing medicine shows, working off and on at the Mobile docks while many of the other men were in uniform, making his first lackadaisical attempts at drying out, reluctant to leave the safety of singing on WSFA and in the surrounding small towns—and the locals were coming to have a gawk at him. There would be a parade downtown, a benefit at the Veterans Administration hospital, and a big show at the new Cow Coliseum starring Hank, supported by Hank Snow and the Carter Family. He taped a promotional spot for WSFA: "When a boy grows up in a town and makes a little name for himself and the folks are nice enough to bring him back and designate a whole day as a homecomin', well, folks couldn't be no nicer. . . ." The city of Greenville would follow with a similar celebration the next summer, when he was on his final downhill slide, but this "how-dee-do," as he called it with some pride, was the first major acknowledgment by the home folks that he had made the big time.

Hank also saw the return to Montgomery as a chance to bring his family together after years of smoldering antagonisms. He would publicly thank Lillie for her help as the aggressive stage mom in his formative years—not getting into her continuing warfare with Audrey—and he made sure that Lon Williams would be there as well. Slowly, over the years, he and his father had circled each other and worked out a relationship that was more like adult acquaintances than father and son. Since his final release from VA hospitals in 1939, when Hank was beginning to make his mark as "the Singing Kid" with his first band on WSFA, Lon had settled into a quiet life in the little town of McWilliams, about eighty miles southwest of Montgomery, with his second wife and their daughter, living on his VA disability checks for the rest of his days. Before his career took him to Shreveport and then Nashville, Hank had made it a point to stop over in McWilliams with his various bands as they worked south Alabama, to visit his father and stepmother and stepsister (introducing himself to her,

Leila, as her "half-a-brother"), trying to build some sort of a relationship. There wasn't much there to build from, of course—Lon had missed Hank's childhood and had long ago been replaced by Fred Rose as a father figure—but they had stayed in touch, no matter how much Lillie tried to keep them apart, and Hank saw the Montgomery homecoming as a way to let the folks know that he did have a father after all.

This was a big deal for the people of Montgomery as well. Except for the goings-on at the state capitol building, not much happened there to attract the outside world beyond a low-rent college football all-star game called the Blue-Gray Game, and big crowds assembled for the parade, madly waving at Hank as he rode in an open convertible in his fringed white cowboy outfit, and cheering for him during the show later in the afternoon at the Cow Coliseum. Inexplicably, Hank had come down from Nashville without a guitar, and his uncle Walter McNeil had to double-park in front of a music store while he went inside to buy one; when they refused to let him pay, he noted the irony: "Ten years ago, when I wanted to buy a damned guitar on credit, they wouldn't let me have it; now they're giving me one." Lillie and Lon and their kin tried to mind their manners during the festivities (although Audrey was seen angrily snatching little Hank, Jr., away from Lon when he tried to hold his grandson for the first time). At Hank's insistence, the Jaycees presented Lillie with a batch of roses and a gold watch. There was music that afternoon, in spite of a new sound system that was found lacking, and Hank surely found some redemption in a town where they still gossiped about Lillie's boardinghouse and her scrawny teenaged son's misadventures. The next time they saw him, only a year and a half later, he would be laid out in a coffin.

·   ·   ·

Audrey and the kids had flown into Montgomery for the day
and they flew right back to Nashville when it was over, leaving
Hank and the Cowboys to spend the night at Lillie's boardinghouse. The place buzzed all night with family, friends, and
fans. All of this had been most satisfying to Hank, a time to
celebrate his roots, but a look at his schedule for the remainder of the year was enough to give him the shivers. The success of Tony Bennett's pop version of "Cold, Cold Heart" had,
indeed, thrown him into another orbit by introducing him to
the world at large. Fred Rose had scheduled three more
recording sessions that year to capitalize on it. Hank had
agreed to put his name on a booklet entitled *Hank Williams
Tells How to Write Folk and Western Music to Sell*, actually written by a private-school math teacher in Nashville, an endeavor
that might have shed light on the Williams-Rose collaboration
had Hank chosen to contribute anything at all to it. Behind the
scenes, negotiations were ongoing for a movie deal with MGM
Pictures. In the waning months of '51, working around the
usual hectic schedule of one-nighters all the way from Louisiana
roadhouses to concert halls up east, he was booked for the
popular network television shows hosted by Kate Smith and
Perry Como. All of that was promising and profitable for his
career in many ways, but there was a dark side. He was a tired
man—on and off the booze, certain by now that Audrey was
working one-nighters of her own with other men during his
long absences, the pain in his back becoming unbearable—
and it seemed only a matter of time before he would collapse
from the pressure.

Compared to all of that, the next chapter in his life looked
like a piece of cake, almost an all-expenses-paid vacation. His

Cajun pal Dudley LeBlanc had hired him to headline what would turn out to be the last great traveling medicine show: the Hadacol Caravan. Only Coca-Cola was spending more advertising dollars on its product than LeBlanc was on his particular elixir, the foul-tasting "patented medicine" laced with alcohol, and this time he was pulling out all the stops. For six weeks, beginning in Lafayette, Louisiana, Hank and some of the other biggest names in entertainment—Bob Hope, Milton Berle, Dick Haymes, Tony Martin, Cesar Romero, Jack Benny, Jimmy Durante, Rudy Vallee, even Jack Dempsey—would roll across eighteen states in the South and Southwest in a string of nineteen Pullman cars. At every stop there would be a parade, and then a spectacular show at a stadium or whatever was the largest venue in town. Admission was one Hadacol box top for kids, two for adults. Unbeknownst to the performers, LeBlanc's empire was crumbling—he had lost $2 million in that quarter of the year alone, the country's fascination with Hadacol had about peaked, and government drug enforcers were on his case—and this was his last-ditch attempt to salvage it. What could Hank care? He was riding the rails in an air-conditioned Pullman rather than being jammed into his Cadillac; eating fancy meals in a club car; having his laundry taken care of daily; free to chase the bevy of long-stemmed dancing girls assigned to the show, and getting paid well to be the star of an extravaganza that was drawing between ten thousand and twenty-five thousand in stadiums. He and Minnie Pearl had made an arrangement to miss the Saturday performances so they could get onto Henry Cannon's plane and fly to Nashville for their performances on the Opry.

He learned early on just how big a star he had become. Most of the other performers had barely heard of Hank

Williams, but soon they and even the California-based dancers were crowding the stages to follow his performances. The Caravan was working in Hank's backyard, from Cajun country to the border states like Kentucky and Missouri, and he was met with tumultuous welcomes at every stop. The truly big names like Hope and Berle had signed on for occasional appearances, and both of those ran afoul of Hank's drawing power. Berle, for example, had tactlessly whipped out a bandanna and begun faking a crying jag for all to see while Haymes sang "Old Man River"; the crowd loved it, but not one of the Cowboys did—they confronted Berle and threatened to break a guitar over his head if he did that when Hank was singing one of his sad songs of unrequited love. What happened to Hope when he was scheduled to follow Hank in Louisville soon topped the list of Hank Stories. Hank had reluctantly agreed to allow Hope top billing that night—after all, this was Bob Hope—but he was going to make him pay. He performed the whole package, from "Lovesick" to "Cold, Cold Heart," and he took so many encores that LeBlanc, serving as master of ceremonies, couldn't introduce Hope over the roar of the crowd. When it finally subsided, Hope shuffled onto the stage, wearing the oversized cowboy hat he had worn in his recent movie *Paleface,* and said, "Just call me Hank Hope." When he finished his monologue he buttonholed LeBlanc and got a promise that he would never have to follow this Hank Williams again.

It was fun while it lasted. They were in Dallas, with a couple of weeks to go, when LeBlanc abruptly announced the Caravan was over. His checks had begun to bounce—Hank's last one was for $7,500—and he had managed to sell the Hadacol franchise for eight-and-a-half million dollars. As it turned out, it was only paper money. Drowning in a sea of lawsuits and government threats, LeBlanc saw profits of only $250,000 from the sale and Hadacol was officially declared bankrupt a year later, ending one of the most bizarre stories of hucksterism in American history. Meanwhile, when the Caravan ended that day in Texas, Hank and Minnie Pearl flew back home to Nashville while a couple of the Drifting Cowboys were dispatched to Lafayette to fetch the Cadillac. They were among the lucky ones; some of the California showgirls, virtually penniless after having regularly mailed their worthless paychecks home, had to ride the rails to the end of the line in Juarez, Mexico, where they then hitched a ride on a cattle car from El Paso to get home to Los Angeles.

Both Gene Autry and Tex Ritter had become wealthy as cowboy movie stars, transcending their status as country singers, and it seemed only a matter of time before Hollywood would go after the hottest property in Nashville. They knew the audiences overlapped—country music fans loved cowboy movies as well—and MGM Pictures, stablemate of MGM Records, had certainly noted that Hank's easygoing manner onstage was a major part of his appeal. *Billboard* and the Nashville newspapers had picked up on the rumors that a deal was in the offing, and Hank seemed to enjoy the possibility of such a move much more than the actual fact, coyly talking about the hours he had spent as a child watching the movies in south Alabama. Those who knew him, though, could only shake their heads when conjuring a vision of Hiram Williams sitting down to "take a meeting" with some tanned movie producer in the distant make-believe kingdom of Hollywood, California. Those old feelings of insecurity were certain to come back again.

Autry and Ritter were different animals—Ritter, although raised in east Texas, had earned a business degree in college and had married a movie actress—but Hank was most at home singing in a roadhouse. He understood that; Hollywood, much to its chagrin, did not.

Thus it was that a deal was announced, backstage at the Ryman Auditorium, on the night of Hank's return to the Opry following the collapse of the Hadacol Caravan. He wouldn't be making horse operas ("oaters" in *Variety* and *Billboard* vernacular) but costarring in real movies with the likes of the luscious swimming star Esther Williams. The contract he signed with MGM Pictures called for four years, paying him about $4,000 dollars a week while on the job, no picture to take more than four weeks of his time, and a guarantee that he would make at least $10,000 per movie. That sounded like good money, but Hank had done the math. He was getting top dollar for working big concerts, and could easily make more money than Hollywood was offering each week by staying on the road, which accounted for the photos taken backstage at the Opry that night to mark the occasion: Wesley Rose and MGM's Frank Walker with cigars, the Drifting Cowboys in their stage costumes, and Hank with a pen in his hand and a cowboy hat on his head and something less than a smile on his face.

Maybe he never really took it seriously. Certainly the old cautions about a poor southern boy's "risin' above your raisin'" were at play, for twice in the coming months Hank managed to sabotage Hollywood's plans to make him a movie star. (Years later, Buck Owens would write a song called "Act Naturally" that might just as well have been about Hank's brush with Hollywood: "They're gonna put me in the movies . . . and all I gotta do is act naturally.") He went to Los

Angeles that fall for a meeting with MGM producer Joe Paster-
nak, who ordered that he be fitted for a toupee, causing Hank
to grumble that it had made him feel like a heifer being prepared for auction. The following spring, back in California
again to seal the deal with MGM, he blew it off once and for
all; liquored up, resenting what he perceived as a condescend-
ing attitude from one of the company's biggest muckety-
mucks, Dore Schary, he sauntered into the office, threw his
boots on Schary's desk, tipped his hat over his eyes, and proceeded to mumble *yeps* and *nopes* throughout the "interview."
He had shown them what they could do with their palm trees.
MGM, in turn, showed Hank what he could do with his imper-
tinence: there was a curt letter awaiting him when he got back
to Nashville, dated the very day after his visit with Schary, "to
notify you that, for good and sufficient cause, your employment
under said contract is hereby terminated."

It had been a bad idea, anyway, and Hank knew it. He was
born to write songs and perform them for live audiences, not to
prance about a movie set, reciting lines written by someone
else. Had he lived long enough to witness the coming of Elvis
Presley, he likely would have delighted in watching Elvis
make an ass of himself in a series of awful low-budget
movies—the singing Elvis as a circus roustabout, as a pris-
oner, as a boxer and a pilot and a race-car driver, ad
nauseam—while he, the humble poet of the common man,
stayed true to his roots. Even though television was a fairly
new medium, one requiring a certain screen presence, Hank
had little difficulty adapting to it in the fall of '51, when he
made his first national TV appearances, because all he had to
do was, well, act naturally. As a guest on both *The Kate Smith
Evening Hour* and *The Perry Como Show* he was introduced,

bantered briefly with the host, and then sang: the same routine
he followed every Saturday night on Prince Albert's portion at
the Opry. Only the presence of television cameras made it any
different from playing just another one-nighter. Indeed, the
week before he was to do the Como show in New York, he was
working the Wagon Wheel Club on the Auburn-Opelika Highway in east Alabama.

As he neared the end of his most successful year, Hank resembled a leaky old boat in need of repairs. He had turned twenty-
eight in September, but the drinking sprees were coming more
often, bringing with them bouts of depression and black nights
full of self-doubts and open warfare with Audrey. He was being
pulled off the road for more incarcerations in sanitariums, in
Shreveport and Montgomery and Nashville and Louisville
(where he was deemed not an alcoholic, just another binge
drinker, exactly what he wanted to hear), and there were times
when it seemed he had lost the will to carry on. "I wish I was
back at WSFA making twelve dollars a week," he told his uncle Walter McNeil from a hospital bed in Montgomery, surly
and paranoid, living unhappily with his success. He spent
some time confiding with Ernest Tubb, a recovering alcoholic,
who told him of one solution—there was a capsule he could
take every morning, Antabuse, but if he took a single sip of
whiskey he would either die from the reaction or wish he
had—and that was the end of that. Everybody else seemed to
be able to blow off steam with a healthy toot—it was a hard-
drinking crowd, the Opry bunch, floating in a sea of whiskey
from one roadhouse to another—so why couldn't he? One
drink would lead to another binge, to drying out in the me-
dieval huts behind the Madison hospital, and the cycle would

continue upon his release. Not eating, or at best eating poorly, had turned him into a 130-pound scarecrow with a twenty-eight-inch waist.

He figured at least he could do something about the back problems that had worsened through the years of riding in cramped cars from date to date. In the spring, while drying out at a hospital in Shreveport, he had been outfitted with a chrome-and-leather back brace, which only led to more discomfort. The last straw came in the fall when he took a catastrophic spill in a ditch while hunting with Jerry Rivers, putting him in excruciating pain, so in late December he checked himself in to the Vanderbilt Medical College in Nashville. "Cure me or kill me," he told the surgeons there. "I can't go on like this." They did the best they could and reluctantly allowed him to go home so he could recover from the surgery during the Christmas holidays on Franklin Road, where all hell promptly broke loose. By now the marriage seemed irretrievably ruptured. Audrey wasn't there much— she was gone most nights, and one day came back empty-handed when she was supposed to have been shopping for Christmas gifts for the kids—and when he arose from his sickbed long enough to throw a chair at her, straining his back, he was sent back to the hospital for more repairs.

Before the surgery, Hank had been booked for some New Year's Eve shows in the Washington-Baltimore area. That was impossible now. Jimmie Davis would take his place, and Audrey, "Mrs. Hank Williams," would go along as well, to sing with the Drifting Cowboys and to play a recorded message from Hank himself. WSM's Jim Denny had insisted that Hank literally go on record with an apology to allay any suspicions that he was simply drunk again. In it, Hank went into painful detail about his back problems: ". . . I had two ruptured discs in my back. The first and second vertebra was no good . . . deformed when I was a child, or wore out or something. [I wanted to] take an airplane with a stretcher in it [but they said] it'd be impossible for me to be out of here before the first of February. . . ."

For Audrey, the week between Christmas and New Year's was like living in a cage with a wounded animal. Hank practically had to crawl between the bedroom and the bathroom. They snarled and threw things at each other, and on the last Saturday of the year she moved herself and the kids to the home of neighbors. On the next morning, New Year's Eve, she sneaked into the house, accompanied by three lady friends (as witnesses, more than anything), to fetch the clothes she would need for the trip to Washington. "We were just easin' around," she would later write, "and I knew he was there and very edgy, and as we were leaving the gun shot four times. I could hardly walk. I was scared to death."

She flew to D.C. and did her duty, singing and playing the tape of Hank's "apology." And then, getting toward midnight on that New Year's Eve, the ringing of the phone echoed through the hollow rooms at 4916 Franklin Road. It was Audrey. "Hank," she said, "I'll never live with you another day."

The Crash

This time, Audrey meant it. Among the songs Hank was piddling with but never finished was one entitled "I'm Gonna Hire a Lawyer," and that refrain was ringing in his head as he got into his car and scuttled home to Montgomery—back to his mother's boardinghouse, always a refuge whenever he couldn't think of anyplace else to go and hide—to curl up in his old bedroom with booze and painkillers for comfort in the cold. By now, having learned how easy it was to stockpile pills from physicians eager to help out "ol' Hank," prescription drugs were as much a part of his baggage as his guitar and boots. Beset by Lillie's clucking and raising hell, he asked his father to come over from McWilliams and rescue him, but Lon got there just in time to see his son being carried out on a stretcher to an ambulance bound for a hospital. Lillie swore that he had swallowed no more than two aspirin tablets and a couple of beers that day, but the doctors told Lon that they couldn't release Hank until they had flushed "the dope" from his frail body. It was some homecoming this time around.

Within a week, Hank was back in Nashville, renting a two-story stone cottage near the Vanderbilt medical center and sharing accommodations with a young Texas singer named Ray Price, and that's when the impending divorce took on a life of its own. Messy marriage, messy divorce. It resembled a soap opera or something from one of Hank's romance magazines. Lawyers were hired, depositions taken, bills of complaint and countercomplaints filed and, as the bile flew, fans and people in the business found themselves choosing sides. It was sordid stuff, the basis for many of Hank's songs about love gone wrong, but there was no occasion for background music this time. First to fire a salvo was Audrey, who listed every "misconduct" she could come up with from their seven-year marriage: the drinking, the cursing, the physical abuse, ending with the holiday shootings that had made cohabitation "unsafe and improper." She sent MGM and Acuff-Rose scurrying to produce Hank's financial records so she could get her share. Hank's cross-complaint, a blend of "Your Cheatin' Heart" and legalese, was even more damning in its specificity. Audrey spent money like crazy, he said, called him a "son of a bitch" and worse, refused her "obligations of married life," was a rotten mother often carousing at night (Hank, Jr., even called his nurse "Mama"), persistently drove a wedge between him and his own mother, insisted on singing when she had "neither voice nor musical ability"; and then, finally, he brought up the abortion and claimed to have evidence that she had carried on affairs with a highway patrolman and a car salesman, to name a couple of them, while he was on the road.

That's the way divorces work in America—you take your best hold, exaggerating if you have to, in order to get the best deal—but for a while there were some indications that maybe this would go away like it did in 1948, when they turned out to be merely separated for a few weeks before coming back together. As bad as the marriage had become, both Hank and Audrey were taking sober looks at the alternative: he would lose his son, his house, at least half of his money, and, worse, any remaining possibility of holding on to the only woman he ever loved; she would become the former Mrs. Hank Williams, just another single mother stuck with two children to raise, and would no longer have unbridled access to their sizable joint checking account. As the proceedings wound their way through the courts, the terms of the settlement taking on the hard clarity of black words on white paper, they both balked at formally agreeing to a divorce. In effect, someone, meaning the court, was going to have to make them do it.

Unable to work since the failed surgery on his back—skulking around the rented house, drinking and jumping into bed with whomever came along, worried sick about his quandary—Hank had to disband the Drifting Cowboys. He hoped the situation would be temporary, that in due time he could bring them all back together, even left one of his cars in a Nashville garage for the day when he might need them to join him, but in the meantime they had families to feed and were forced to take whatever came along: signing on with Ray Price or Carl Smith, or dropping out of music altogether. When he finally did attempt a return to the stage, on the last weekend of January in '52, he was in no condition for it. The place was Richmond, Virginia, where he was to headline shows on successive nights, and the first thing he did upon checking into a hotel was to order up a jug of tomato juice. Closely guarded to keep him off the sauce, by now willing to settle for anything that would give him a buzz, he asked the room-service waiter to bring him some rubbing alcohol so he could "treat a bad leg." The moment it arrived, he made himself a monster Bloody Mary and promptly began throwing up the whole mess. The one beer he was allowed to have before the show, in hopes it would settle him down enough to perform, didn't do much good. He proceeded to make an utter fool of himself, and to make it worse there was a newspaper reporter in the crowd.

His new roommate back in Nashville, Ray Price, was the opening act. When he finished performing and gave Hank a grand introduction, the anxious crowd grew testy the moment they saw him struggle to the microphone, obviously too drunk to stand upright, and they were aghast when they heard Hank forget the words and even the key of the one song he tried before abruptly weaving offstage. The emcee jumped in, trying to calm the crowd, saying Hank wasn't feeling well, that Price would sing some of his songs and anybody not satisfied could get a refund. Meanwhile, during intermission, his guard was stuffing Hank with a sandwich and coffee, forcing him to walk around in the cold night air. When Hank was brought on for the second show, neither drunk nor sober but in that in-between stage of defensiveness, he was anything but apologetic. Hank Williams was no liar, he told them, and he would be glad to show his surgery scars to anybody who doubted he was hurting, and "if you ain't nice to me, I'll turn around and walk right off." Ray Price stepped in to do the best he could, begging the crowd to applaud—"We all love you, Hank, don't we, folks?"—and Hank responded by meandering through some of his songs. The man who never met a fan he didn't like promptly left when it was over, going straight to his Cadillac.

It was all over the *Richmond Times-Dispatch* the next morning, under a headline reading "Hank Williams Hillbilly Show Is Different: Star Makes Impression of Unexpected Kind." The reporter, Edith Lindeman (an erstwhile songwriter who later would coauthor Kitty Kallen's hit, "Little Things Mean a Lot") didn't leave anything out. This was in the days when the press was more benign, paying little attention to live shows, so Hank and the other members of the troupe were startled to read such detailed coverage of a performance that had gone badly wrong. That night, Hank won back the crowd—*didn't he always?*—when he stepped to the microphone and said he was dedicating his first tune to "a gracious lady writer," promptly leading his backup band into "Mind Your Own Business." It was a lively show, and afterward he signed autographs for his forgiving fans, the ones privy to his troubles with Audrey who were inclined to say the man had every right to drink, before getting into the limo to ride to his next adventure.

And so it went during the early months of '52, with more lows than highs. Caught in the middle of the caterwauling between Hank and Audrey, or at least having a ringside seat as the drama unfolded, were the surviving members of the Original Carter Family. Eck and Mother Maybelle Carter and their beautiful singing daughters, Helen and June and Anita, were the most revered members of the Opry—the First Family, as it were, sturdy country people whose recordings in 1927 had opened the doors for the commercialization of country music—and they were at once appalled and mesmerized by Hank. He had latched on to them early in his Nashville days, admiring their music and their familial ways, as though he wanted them to be his surrogate family. He was a regular visitor at their house, hunkering over plates of homemade biscuits and gravy or spooning from bowls of corn bread crumbled in milk, like a whimpering dog that had come in from the rain. Maybelle was the mother he wished he'd had, firm but nonjudgmental, and he called her "Mama."

Hank had developed a fixation on the prettiest of the daughters, Anita, a tall brunette with a classic Appalachian soprano voice. Only a teenager, probably a virgin, and certainly one who had never even tasted whiskey, she didn't quite know what to make of his advances. On the night Hank introduced "Cold, Cold Heart" at the Opry, she had stood offstage with tears streaming down her face ("I thought it was the saddest and most beautiful thing I'd ever heard"), and when Hank asked her out on a date she said yes, but only if the whole family could go along, which they did. He was still in hot pursuit in April of '52 when he and the Carters went to New York to appear on Kate Smith's network television show. (Hank and Anita's duet of "I Can't Help It if I'm Still in Love with You" is the single greatest piece of film of Hank in his prime.) Hank had given Anita a ring and said he would take her anywhere she wanted to go in New York. When the girl from the Clinch Mountains of Virginia said she had always wanted to hear Peggy Lee sing at the Copacabana, off they went. Lee happened to be singing one of Hank's songs when they walked in, and soon the two were on the dance floor, Hank embarrassing Anita by kicking his bony knees waist-high, doing the Texas Two-Step. The sophisticated New Yorkers in the crowd were having a good laugh and could hardly believe it when Lee introduced the skeletal hillbilly in the gray double-breasted suit as the great Hank Williams.

Nothing came of the romance, but the Carters weren't rid of Hank. As the divorce proceedings continued between their friends, they bore the brunt of his jealousies and antagonisms toward Audrey—drunkenly calling Anita in the middle of the night for commiseration, crying on Maybelle's shoulder, once even trying to ram a car he thought held Audrey and June—and June, especially, tried to shame him on moral grounds. Her greatest contribution to American music, after all, would be to extend the life of another tortured wastrel, Johnny Cash, during the thirty-five years of their fabled marriage. The last straw came when June, trying to mediate a fight between Hank and Audrey, literally got caught in the line of fire: in the driveway of the house on Franklin Road, a drunken Hank fired a pistol at Audrey but missed June's head by six inches, temporarily deafening her and dropping her to the ground out of sheer fright. "You've killed June! You've killed June!" Audrey shouted, and Hank's response was to jump into his car and speed away. His distraught apology to June a week later did little good. "I realized he really was crazy," June said. "We knew he was going to die, and he was going to die soon."

He had managed to avoid trouble during the trip to New York, partly by staying in his guarded room at the Hotel Astor on Times Square and composing the lyrics for a song that would never be published or recorded, "You'll Never Again Be Mine." For obvious reasons, New York City wasn't his kind of place, any more than the next stop on his calendar, the West Coast. He had flown out for some dates in California, and since he was there it was time to finalize the deal with MGM Pictures. (Fred Rose's son Wesley was with Hank that next spring when he threw his boots on Dore Schary's desk to completely blow off any chances he would ever have to make motion pictures.) He had warmed up for that dreaded meeting with a few belts of whiskey, and by the time he was to headline a show in San Diego a couple of days later he was drunk again. Minnie Pearl was a part of the troupe, and she remembered how when Hank messed up on the first show she and some others were asked to drive him around during intermission in hopes of sobering him up: "We started singing. He was all hunkered down, looking out of the side of the car, singing, 'I Saw the Light,' and then he stopped and he turned around, and his face broke up and he said, 'Minnie, I don't see no light. There ain't no light.'"

The *other* California, the Bay Area, was more to his liking, especially Oakland with its surrounding blue-collar towns populated by southern expatriates who had come to work the factories during the Second World War. He was booked into several classic roadhouses in the area, and on the day of his checking in to a hotel in Oakland he was met by one of the few big-city reporters who would ever interview him. Ralph J. Gleason was with the *San Francisco Chronicle* and years later would recount the meeting for *Rolling Stone*: "Hank Williams came out of the bathroom carrying a glass of water. He was lean, slightly stooped over, and low-jawed. He shook hands quickly, then went over to the top of the bureau, swept off a handful of pills and deftly dropped them, one at a time, with short, expert slugs from the glass." Gleason admitted knowing little about country music, which Hank was calling "folk" music at the time ("When a folk singer sings a sad song, he's sad"), only that Hank "wrote good songs" and had gotten rich from it. They repaired to the hotel coffee shop to continue the interview over breakfast. Hank revealed little that we don't know now; telling Gleason about south Alabama and "this old Nigrah" named Tee-Tot, about WSFA and getting paid ninety dollars for cutting four sides in his first recording session with Sterling, and about the Opry. Acuff was his idol, he said, Fred Rose his inspiration, and he really liked the way Johnny Ray belted out "Cry."

That night, at seedy San Pablo Hall, about thirty miles north of downtown Oakland, Hank was in his element. "You parked in the mud and walked past a tree up to the door" of a white one-story cinderblock building, Gleason wrote, "and inside there was a long room with a bandstand at one end and a bar in an annex at one side." It was Thigpen's Log Cabin all over again. The beer and whiskey flowed and the people danced until Hank sang. "There were lots of those blondes you see at C&W affairs, the kind of hair that Mother never had and nature never grew and the tight skirts that won't quit and the guys looking barbershop-neat but still with a touch of dust on them." This newcomer to the music could see that Hank "had that *thing*. He made them scream when he sang [as though they had been] shipped right up from Enid or Wichita Falls," and he sang everything he knew. By intermission, Hank "was a little stoned and didn't seem to remember our conversation earlier in the day and the party was beginning to get a little rough," so Gleason left. Six months later, reading of Hank's death, he remembered his passionate singing—"He didn't cry but he made *you* cry, and when he sang 'Lovesick Blues' you knew he meant it"—and his dream to retire to his farm and "watch them cattle work while I write songs and fish."

The road was getting longer and harder as the Opry tried mightily to capitalize on its biggest star—from California he went to Boston's Symphony Hall, to Canada, and to Texas— until, finally, he was booked into Las Vegas, not without a great deal of trepidation on all sides. *Hank? In Vegas? Please.* It was an ill-advised venture, on many counts. Then, as now, the successful Vegas acts are the ones that can offer painless entertainment—showgirls, stand-up comics, Wayne Newton, Elvis—not some brokenhearted hillbilly poet who will divert the high-rollers from their drinking, gambling, and womanizing. By now the chances were down to fifty-fifty that Hank would be sober. He was scheduled for two weeks at the Last Frontier, fronting for an old vaudevillian. Hank had managed to hire Don Helms and Jerry Rivers for the gig, and the Opry's Jim Denny ordered them to drive Hank all the way from Nashville to Vegas and to hire minders to guard him around the clock once they got there. It was a disaster from beginning to end—Hank didn't like seeing a sea of dressed-up patrons in the audience any more than they liked what they were seeing and hearing on the stage—and the show was canceled after one week. "The closer we got to Vegas, the more nervous he became," Helms said of the drive out, and when Hank learned of the cancellation, "I could see a sigh of relief come over him." The only people who had enjoyed it were the random ranchers and fans of country and western, virtual strangers to nightclubs, who tended to nurse a beer through the show and bypass the gaming tables on their way out. Hank began drinking the minute he was fired, and he got seriously wasted in the backseat of the limo while Helms and Rivers took turns at the wheel on the long drive across the country through the blazing summer sun. At least when he got home he wouldn't have to explain anything to Audrey.

Everything else might be collapsing around him, but there was always the studio: his haven, his comforter, increasingly the only place where he felt truly at home and safe from the monsters that haunted him. No matter what, through hell and high water, nearly every record he cut now was hitting the charts—most recently "Baby, We're Really in Love," "Honky Tonk Blues," "Half as Much," "Cold, Cold Heart," "Hey, Good Lookin'"—and on a Friday the thirteenth in June he was back at Castle Studio, for the first time in six months, to record four more records that would join the Hank Williams canon. Only "Jambalaya" was truly Hank's concoction, with a lot of help on the patois from his Cajun friends, but the others certainly were tailored for him. "Window Shopping," a lighthearted lament ("you're only shopping for love"), had been written by a French-born newspaper artist in New York; the songwriting credits of "Settin' the Woods on Fire" were shared by Fred Rose and a friend who, incidentally, had introduced him to Christian Science; and Hank split the credits with Fred for writing "I'll Never Get Out of This World Alive." The latter was the final cut of the afternoon, at the end of a three-hour session, and Hank was so weak that he had to take a seat in a chair between the many takes required to finally get it right. Whatever the circumstances, "Jambalaya" would turn out to be the biggest commercial hit of his career.

It was on the next night, at the Opry, that he met the woman he determined would become his second wife. A promising singer from the Louisiana Hayride, Faron Young, was making a guest appearance and was accompanied by a curvaceous teenaged beauty with flaming red hair and bounteous breasts. Hank's eyes popped out when he saw her sitting in the backstage glass cubicle reserved for guests of the performers, wearing a tight-fitting off-the-shoulder dress revealing Gibson Girl cleavage he could only dream of, and he homed in on her. She was Billie Jean Jones, from Shreveport, currently Young's girlfriend, and she called Hank "sir" when he began making his inquiries. Smitten, Hank summoned Young to the cubicle and asked what his intentions were. "She's got too many boyfriends, Hank. I can't keep up with her," Young told him. Hank pointed out a beauty on the front row, "that ol' black-haired gal in the front row with the red dress on," a groupie who had come all the way from Pennsylvania to be with him, and proposed that they switch women for a night on the town after the show. When they reached a nightclub, Billie Jean wouldn't go inside—she didn't drink, she said, was tired from traveling all day, and she wasn't so naïve that she didn't know of Hank's reputation—and so the two of them stayed in Faron's car and talked. He found out she had a child, was separated from the father, lived with her parents, and was working as a telephone operator for the phone company in Shreveport. And this: she said that when Hank and Audrey had a house in Bossier City in '49, during his Hayride days, she lived four doors away and always told her mother she was going to marry Hank Williams someday.

Oh, the women in his life! Any day now he expected to hear the word that his marriage to Audrey was officially over. He had just learned that he had impregnated a comely young woman named Bobbie Jett, a dancer-cum-secretary known well around music circles in Nashville, and he couldn't get rid of her. Now he thought he was in love again, with Billie Jean. Between that and the drinking and the incessant back pain, his life was becoming more unmanageable by the day. The house he was renting had become a magnet for has-beens and wannabes—*Party Time!*—a place where the booze flowed, women ran amok, and songs were sung; where Hank, always afraid of being alone, would sit on the floor in the middle of the traffic, glumly pretending to write songs. It got so bad that Ray Price, living in the upstairs quarters, packed up his stuff and moved out. Concerned that this time Hank really was intent on drinking himself to death, Price and Don Helms had the people from the Madison sanitarium come to sedate him and drag him away to the dreaded "huts" for his own protection.

The divorce became final on July 10. Because he had contested little in the preliminary agreements, in the futile hope that Audrey might back out at the last minute, Hank got burned. Audrey would get half of his future earnings, the house on Franklin Road, $1,000 in cash, her Cadillac convertible, and custody of three-year-old "Bocephus," Hank, Jr. Hank paid her attorney's fees, was ordered to pay for his son's support until he turned twenty-one, and got only the failing store downtown and the forsaken farm in Franklin. There was no savings account to be divided. Even so, it was a gamble on Audrey's part because no one had any way of knowing for sure what "future royalties" there would be, given the rate of Hank's decline; and if she ever remarried she would lose all claims to any royalties and be reduced to receiving basic child support.

To no one's surprise, Hank charged into the studio on the very next afternoon and came out firing the only way he knew how. He cut four sides in only two hours, two of them "Luke the Drifter" recitations, and was out of there with an hour left of paid-up studio time. The material might have been maudlin in any other performer's hands, but not when it was Hank Williams reading from his notes as though to say *Here's what the bitch done to me*. First out of the box came "You Win Again," arguably the saddest lament he ever wrote ("You have no heart, you have no shame. . . ."), with knowing nods in the studio from his pals Jerry Rivers and Don Helms, who had lived through it all with Hank. Then came a decidedly un-Hank tune called "I Won't Be Home No More," a jaunty in-your-face good-bye in which he seemed to be shooting his middle finger to Audrey: "I used to be the patient kind, believed each alibi / but that's all done, I've changed my mind, I've got new fish to fry. . . ." As Luke the Drifter, he intoned someone else's lyrics in "Be Careful of Stones That You Throw," a defiant response to the swelling ranks of fans and bookers clucking about his wayward ways; and then ended the session with a point-blank shot at Audrey in "Please Make Up Your Mind": "My life with you has been one hard knock / Lord, my head looks like an old chop block. . . ." He would see Castle Studio only one more time.

At the Opry, the very next night, Hank's mood was almost carefree, as though he had finally gotten rid of some bad juices. The interplay between him and Red Foley, the emcee of the networked Prince Albert tobacco portion, was downright jocular. "I got a brand-new song that ain't never been aired," said Hank. "Ain't never been aired?" Foley said, following the rehearsed script. "No, and it might need airin'." *That Hank, ain't he something?* The people who were crammed into the Ryman, trying to stir the air of a stultifying July night with their funeral-parlor fans, howled at Hank's droll backwoods humor and wiggled into their slick church-pew seats. "It's 'Jam-bal-*eye*-oh on the *Beye*-oh.'" Then, on one of the last nights he would ever play the Opry, Hank waited for the upbeat intro from Don Helms's steel guitar before jumping into the tune that had been laying 'em out all over Louisiana and Texas—"Good-bye, Joe, me gotta go . . ."—and if he didn't get the same tumultuous reaction as he had in his Opry debut with "Lovesick Blues" it was close. Nobody knew it at the time, and Hank wasn't done quite yet, but it was just about over. That musty old tabernacle, the Mother Church of Country Music, would never see anything like him again.

On a Monday in early August, into his cups, Hank sat in his house and pondered his latest mess. He thought he had successfully wooed Billie Jean—she had taken a room in a boardinghouse in Nashville and gone to work for the Nashville phone company, he had ridden with her to meet her parents in Shreveport, and they had agreed to marry sometime in October—but she had gotten enough of his drinking and his women ("I ain't putting up with this crap no more") and gone back home to Louisiana. Bobbie Jett was still coming around, now beginning to show her pregnancy, and he felt guilty over that. Audrey was refusing to let him see Hank, Jr. Hank and Audrey's Corral and the farm near Franklin were the last things on his mind. He didn't even have a car, having somehow "lost" a Cadillac. Since that last appearance on the Opry a month earlier, when he performed "Jambalaya," he had missed so many radio shows and tour dates that WSM's Jim Denny had warned him that it was all he could do to keep the station from firing him.

When the phone rang that morning, August 11, Denny was on the line. Hank had failed to appear at the Opry the Saturday night before and at a show the following day—the last straw—and that was it. He was fired. "You can't fire me, 'cause I already quit," Hank said. Denny told Hank this was the hardest thing he had ever done in his life, and held out some hope: "Call me in December, and I'll let you know about coming back to the Opry next year." Johnnie Wright, Kitty Wells's husband, happened to be there with Hank, and Denny told Wright to bring him by the station so he could pick up a last check, for about $300. With the word of Hank's dismissal spreading like a brushfire—Don Helms and his wife, Hazel, close friends since the war years, rushed over to return a watch and a shotgun they had been holding and to say good-bye—Hank and Wright began loading up Johnnie's borrowed Chrysler limousine. They took the jump seat out of the limo and replaced it with a recliner from the house, and hitched up the little aluminum trailer with *Hank Williams & the Drifting Cowboys* painted on the side. Johnnie driving, Hank riding in the recliner like a deposed king, they ran by WSM to get the check. "Pull in there and get me some whiskey," Hank said when he saw a liquor store on Broadway, so Wright went inside to get the check cashed and buy a fifth. "Hank out there?" said the clerk. A small knot of people had gathered outside, attracted by the limo pulling Hank's trailer, and they were the last people in Nashville to say farewell to the drifting cowboy.

Down familiar old U.S. 31 they rode out of the undulating hills of middle Tennessee, through Chattanooga and Huntsville and Birmingham, onto the flat pasturelands and cotton fields of south Alabama—surely listening to Hank's own songs on the radio, maybe "Honky Tonk Blues" or "Cold, Cold Heart," for he was everywhere on the dial—finally rolling up to Lillie's boardinghouse in Montgomery. Hank was passed out, drunk, in the recliner, and it took both his mother and Johnnie to drag his wasted body from the limo and carry him inside to the front bedroom downstairs, which had always been "Hank's room." They peeled off his boots and clothes, put him in a pair of pajamas, and slipped him between the sheets. There, he slept.

He awoke the next morning as though nothing had happened. After all, Eddy Arnold was the biggest-selling performer out of Nashville and had done it without having to hustle back to the Opry every other Saturday night and perform for peanuts. Back in Nashville, although the news of his firing was in the *Tennessean* and the *Banner*, the Opry was saying only that he

was "sick," an old story that nobody was buying anymore, and
the kindly Montgomery papers were reporting "blood poison-
ing" from an infected wound. What Hank needed most right
now was a car, and within a couple of days he had one: a shiny
used powder-blue Cadillac convertible he had bought on time
in Nashville and had someone drive down to Alabama. On Friday morning, he and his mother got into the car and rode fifty
miles down U.S. 31 to Greenville, where another Hank homecoming was to be held. Even though the Williamses had lived
there for only two years, and Greenville never would lay claims
on Hank as a favorite son, crowds totaling some 8,500 would
line the streets for a parade and fill the high school football
stadium for two shows. He made sure that his father was there,
but it was Lillie who rode in the backseat of the new convertible while Hank—dressed in a fringed white "buckskin" outfit
and a cowboy hat, visible bruises showing on his face—
dutifully waved back at the crowd from the shotgun seat. At
the stadium, the site of his spanking as a lackadaisical
teenager by an incensed coach, he paid homage to Rufus "Tee-
Tot" Payne (dead since '39, unbeknownst to Hank, and in an
unmarked pauper's grave in Montgomery), and then he performed like a prodigal son.

The lost Cadillac was found in Philadelphia, returned to
Nashville, and Hank got one of his old band members from
the WSFA days to drive him up to fetch it. While there, they
ran by Bobbie Jett's apartment in order to bring her back to
live at Lillie's place for the remainder of her pregnancy.
"Now," as biographer Colin Escott put it, "Hank had one girlfriend [not counting Billie Jean in Shreveport], two cars, no
band, no show dates, and far too much time on his hands."
Lillie, recognizing this, had arranged for Hank and Bobbie to

spend a few days at a cabin on Lake Martin, east of Montgomery, situated near a slough known as Kowaliga Bay. Hank
wound up spending his first night there in the jail at Alexan-
der City, the result of his being spotted by fans and being
given a jug of moonshine whiskey, but in the next few days at
the cabin he managed to work on two of his greatest songs:
"Your Cheatin' Heart" and "Kaw-Liga," the latter inspired by
a wooden cigar-store Indian totem he had seen at a crossroads
store. He was particularly excited about the prospects for
"Kaw-Liga"—coming back from a night run to a bootlegger's
shanty in the backwoods, he was beating out a tom-tom sound
on the car's dashboard, repeating the opening lyrics, "Kaw-
Liga was a wooden Indian, standing by the door . . ."—so
much so that he called Fred Rose in Nashville with a request
that he get himself down to Montgomery so they could refine
the arrangements.

Fred arrived, and he and Hank set to work in the downstairs front room of the boardinghouse. "Cheatin' Heart"
needed little fixing, but Rose put his fingerprints all over
"Kaw-Liga": filling out the story of a wooden Indian's unrequited love for "an Indian maid down by the antique store,"
and most importantly determining that the opening should be
in a minor key before switching to a major key for the driving
upbeat bridge ("Poor ol' Kaw-Liga, he never got a kiss . . .").
But Fred had bigger plans in mind for the biggest star in
Acuff-Rose's stable. He felt there was a way to get him back on
track. "Jambalaya" was selling briskly, 200,000 copies already, and he used that as a wedge when he began talking to
Horace Logan at KWKH about reinstating Hank on the
Louisiana Hayride. Within days, the deal was set. Unloading
Hank and Audrey's Corral and the five-hundred-acre farm at

great losses, Hank cleared Nashville for the last time and
headed west to salvage his career and to reunite with Billie
Jean, the latest love of his life.

It had come to this for the acknowledged king of country music, whose "Jambalaya" was at the top of the country charts.
Everything Hank owned was in the two Cadillacs he and a
friend drove in tandem to Shreveport. Billie Jean had gotten
him a room at a run-down resident motel, "a horrible, horrible" place, furnished with a kitchen table and not much else,
said the promoter Oscar Davis, who had agreed to rejoin Hank.
"He wanted me to meet Billie," Davis said, "so every night we
had to go out and sit and drink." Hank had talked his way into
getting $200 a show on the Louisiana Hayride, compared to
the $18 he was being paid when he left for the Opry more than
three years earlier, and his fans were eagerly awaiting his return to the stage of the Municipal Auditorium. Even so, try as
he might, he couldn't put together a band due to his inconsis-
tency. There were no more huge concerts scheduled in places
like Boston and D.C. and Dallas, just one-nighters in roadhouses and school auditoriums around the Southwest, and he
was back to using house bands who counted on his strumming
the key to begin a song and stomping his foot to signify the
end. Those who still believed in him, or at least had a stake in
his future, saw a blessing in these diminished circumstances:
if he screwed up, not many would hear about it. On the night of
his twenty-ninth birthday, working a dance hall in San Anto-
nio, an eleven-year-old steel guitar prodigy was called to the
stage to sit on Hank's lap and play "Steel Guitar Rag," and the
kid never got over it: "His breath stank of whiskey, and there
wasn't nothin' left to him."

A week later, following his return to the Hayride, Hank was back at Castle Studio in Nashville for what would turn out to be his last recording session. He and Billie Jean had flown in from Shreveport, and Hank had to do some explaining when, lo and behold, the pregnant Bobbie Jett somehow showed up in the studio as well. The faithful Don Helms was there with his steel guitar, as always, with young Chet Atkins on the electric guitar, and in barely more than two hours they would help churn out three records that would live forever. Hank began by cutting a tune he had written for Billie Jean, "I Could Never Be Ashamed of You" (as he was of you-know-who), and then sandwiched the megahit "Kaw-Liga" around two songs that would come to define his tortured life with Audrey: "Your Cheatin' Heart" and "Take These Chains from My Heart." Fans and students of Hank were surprised to learn that the latter was written not by Hank but by Fred Rose and Hy Heath, who had written "Mule Train," but "Cheatin' Heart" clearly came from the depths of Hank's very soul. He was about to fall apart on that day in the studio—skinny as a spider, suffering from chest pains, nearing impotence, incontinent to the point he was wetting his bed every night—and yet when he sang "you'll cry and cry, and try to sleep" it was enough to break anyone's heart. "Nobody had a talent for making suffering enjoyable like Hank Williams," the songwriter Kris Kristofferson would say twenty years later, of Hank's portfolio in general but "Cheatin' Heart" in particular.

In a very real way, it was as though Hank was kissing off a world that had been hurtful from the beginning. If only Audrey and Lillie had been present in the studio for the last session, joining Billie Jean and Bobbie, it might have resembled a hillbilly version of the Last Supper: the martyr, surrounded by the women he had loved to one degree or another, saying a last bittersweet good-bye while death was at his door. When the sales from this final session were tallied and added to all the rest, Hank would have sold an astonishing ten million records in a recording career spanning little more than five years. That was in the middle of the twentieth century, when America was a much smaller place, before sophisticated mass-market schemes placed the "product" in the laps of "consumers" with ever-increasing expendable incomes. He was, in a sense, hand-selling one record at a time through appearances at one-nighters in roadhouses and high school football stadiums and small-town auditoriums. Hank recorded a total of sixty-six songs, thirty-seven of them making the *Billboard* charts, and the most important number is that he had written fifty of them himself. By contrast, Elvis Presley never wrote a song. Two blue-collar country performers who did were Merle Haggard and Johnny Cash, each of them making records during lives that lasted far beyond Hank's twenty-nine years, but they couldn't come close to reaching Hank's percentage of hits.

Before he prepared for one of the biggest shows of his career, his own wedding, there were a couple of pieces of business to take care of. Billie Jean was still officially married to the young airman who had fathered her child, so Hank paid a lawyer to start the divorce proceedings. All along, he had been paying for Bobbie Jett's upkeep at one of Lillie's boardinghouses in Montgomery, but now it was time to face up to responsibility for the child she was due to deliver early in '53. Although the wording of the agreement he had drawn up was contradictory ("Hank Williams *may* be the father of said child" later referred to "the father, Hank Williams"), he clearly was feeling his obligations when he flew to Montgomery and signed papers specific to the point of giving Bobbie a one-way plane ticket to California, without the baby, thirty days after its birth. Both Hank and Bobbie would have visitation rights while the child lived with Lillie and her husband, Bill Stone, and Hank would assume custody from age three to age five, when custody would be shared. Though heavy with child, Bobbie had been popping up at concerts and even at the recording session that day in Nashville, and the heat was on for Hank to get rid of her before he married Billie Jean.

In New Orleans, a town that appreciates ceremony, this must have looked like the wedding of the year. Oscar Davis had concocted not one ceremony but two—a rehearsal in the afternoon and the real thing at night, at the Municipal Auditorium, admission ranging from $1 to $2.80, music by some Hayride members and Hank himself—and had talked a handful of retailers into kicking in some wedding gifts. Hank had invited Audrey to the wedding, out of pure spite, but when he began thinking she might really show up and cause a scene he and Billie and another couple drove thirty miles east of Shreveport to the town of Minden, following the Saturday night Hayride, for a civil ceremony with a justice of the peace, just to be sure. (They had borrowed a '50 Ford from Billie's brother, to throw Audrey off the scent in case she came and tried to ambush them, and they ran out of gas on the way back. Hank stood on the side of the road in his white cowboy outfit, hitching a ride, and when they were picked up he grandly invited the driver to spend the night with them, on their wedding night, but Billie squashed the idea.) The bride and groom flew into New Orleans on the morning of the big day, Sunday the nineteenth of October, and checked into the Jung Hotel on Canal

Street, where Hank began drinking to celebrate. They had to rustle up another preacher when the one originally hired balked, on the grounds that they had already been officially married. A sellout crowd of seven thousand paying customers attended the matinee "rehearsal," and the house was full again for the real thing that night. The Hayride's Billy Walker had barely begun singing "Anything Your Heart Desires" when there was a commotion behind him. Hank, in a dark cowboy suit and white hat, was coming toward him, dragging along Billie Jean in her elaborate white wedding dress. "When ol' Hank comes to git married," he said, "he wants to git married." It was showtime. They were married (again), Hank sang "I Could Never Be Ashamed of You," and they would have flown to Cuba for their honeymoon if he hadn't passed out from the champagne stashed backstage. Audrey, the only person from Nashville on the invitation list, was a no-show.

The newly minted couple, Mr. and Mrs. Hank Williams, moved into a house in a new subdivision in Bossier City, the same suburb where they once had lived separate lives only four doors from each other; he as the swaggering star of the Hayride, she as a dreamy teenager. Billie Jean did the best she could: "He had never been held. I knew I had to be a lover and a mother to him. We wrestled, had picnics. I gave him a childhood. We held hands, and I'd sit on his lap. I wore short-shorts and T-shirts tied up in the front." Unlike Audrey, she had no aspirations toward show business ("All I wanted was him"). She traveled with him when she could, always being proudly introduced to the crowd, and Hank loved it when she strolled through hotel lobbies barefoot like a Daisy Mae. Hank's weight and composure were wildly fluctuating, and he always looked healthier when he had eschewed whiskey long enough for Bil-

lie's mother to fatten him up with some home cooking. Billie
tried to ration the booze, one beer before a show and "two of the
coldest ones you ever had" afterward, but that didn't last very
long. Few people beyond the experts—sociologists, psychologists, and health-care workers—have much of an idea of how to
deal with an alcoholic, and Billie was in over her head.

Early in October, a week or so before the wedding, Hank
had met a man he thought was the answer to his problems. He
was in Oklahoma City for a Hayride package show, drinking
and complaining of chest pains, when somebody told him of
one Horace Raphol "Toby" Marshall, a "doctor" who special-
ized in treating alcoholics. After serving two prison terms, for
armed robbery and then for passing a forged check, Toby Marshall had bought a bogus diploma and set himself up as an alcoholic therapist, vowing as a recovering alcoholic to devote
himself "as unselfishly as possible to helping others as I
could." He was a quack, no doubt about it, conveniently
equipped with official-looking prescription pads. Commiserat-
ing with Hank as one alcoholic to another, Marshall convinced
Hank that he could be cured through empathy and pills. The
trouble was, the drug he had in mind was chloral hydrate, a
powerful sedative that could be fatal when mixed with alcohol
(it was used, in fact, for making Mickey Finns). Hank bought
the whole act and hired Marshall to be his personal physician,
on a $300-a-week retainer. He had found the ultimate enabler,
a doctor who could get him any drug he needed for whatever
ailed him, whether it be the bad back or the chest pains or the
plain old lonesomes.

Through November and into December, the final months of his
life, it was as though Hank was riding a roller coaster to hell.

The travel was grueling—the gulf coast, east Texas, southern Louisiana—and he would be cold sober for a week before "somebody got to him," as the bookers and performers explained it, and he fell off the wagon. Tommy Hill, a fiddler who traveled with Hank during much of that time, said, "He didn't miss that many shows. If somebody said, 'We've got a show to do today,' he wouldn't drink, but if somebody slipped him a drink it was all over. He'd wilt, just wilt from booze. His blood was full of alcohol and he couldn't drink anymore. He was a sick man. When he crossed the line, he was a tyrant; the language, the lack of respect for anybody. He knew he had a problem, but he couldn't leave it alone." A couple of times, Hank's drunken misbehavior nearly led to riots: the night when Hank responded to jeers by saying, "Now you've seen ol' Hank," and leaving the scene; and another time in a Catholic school auditorium when the crowd came up on the stage to get him and chased him to the limo before he managed to escape with the aid of the police. He began missing dates at the Hayride, or showing up drunk, testing the patience of even Horace Logan. Three times in the first eight weeks of the marriage to Billie Jean, Hank was admitted to the North Louisiana Sanitarium in Shreveport.

Two days after getting out of the sanitarium again, on Saturday night, December 13, Hank performed at the Hayride. Immediately after the show, he got into a Pontiac coupe with Tommy and Goldie Hill, brother and sister, who were headed toward Houston to begin a series of dates. He was scrunched down in the backseat, drinking, and Tommy was paying no attention to his passenger until he heard a frightening growl. He looked back to see that Hank had passed out, his head between his knees, and wasn't breathing. They were in the middle of Nacogdoches, Texas, at two o'clock in the morning. "Goldie was hysterical. I stopped the car, dragged Hank out, stood him up, grabbed him around the waist, and began bouncing him up and down until he started breathing. The windpipe had been cut off." Hill had unconsciously performed what amounted to the Heimlich maneuver, opening the air passage so Hank could breathe. They drove on to Houston and dropped Hank at the Rice Hotel.

He was supposed to work Cook's Hoedown Club in Houston that night, but he had continued drinking and switched hotels, and nobody could find him. Panic set in. Toby Marshall was summoned from Oklahoma City, as was the booker out of Austin, and when they finally found him drunk at another hotel they went to work on him: Marshall gave him some beer, injected a drug that made him throw it up, poured some black coffee in him, then gave him some Dexedrine tablets. Before a sellout crowd, Hank was booed off the stage. At intermission they pumped him full of coffee, but he was booed off the stage again. He called Billie Jean and told her he had never been sicker. In Victoria, Texas, on Tuesday, he had what might have been a heart attack and missed the show entirely. This time, the handlers called Lillie in Montgomery and had her flown in to see what she could do. Hank began to come around, performing at a huge hall in Dallas on Wednesday and at a roadhouse in Snook on Thursday, and Lillie was with him in the car as the troupe rolled into Austin for a big show on Friday that would close the brief tour before they were to head back to Shreveport for the Saturday night Hayride.

What happened the night at the Skyline Club became the stuff of legend. The only advertising had been the usual country-radio spots and a one-column ad in the local paper, but a sellout crowd of about one thousand was lining the walls when the curtains opened. Lillie and Toby Marshall, new best friends united in trying to save Hank, were in the audience. Hank wasn't in the best of shape—disheveled, sweating copiously, his nose running from a cold he'd had for weeks—but he was sober and pumped. Tommy Hill performed, then his sister Goldie, and it was while the Texas singer Billy Walker was doing his show that Hank began prodding Tommy, the emcee: "Get him off, get him off, I'm ready to go on." Normally, Hank would have performed a forty-five-minute medley that would lead to the intermission. But there would be no intermission this night. Once he strolled onto the stage and bent over the microphone, strumming his guitar, weaving like a cobra, they couldn't get him off. He sang every song he knew—more than once, if the bellowing crowd wanted it—going for three solid hours without a break. "It was," Tommie Hill said, "the best show I ever witnessed." It was also Hank Williams's last hurrah.

Lost Highway

Not wanting to linger in Austin after the show, Hank and Lillie made the six-hour drive to Shreveport through the bleak stretches of east Texas, arriving in time to awaken Billie Jean in the early-morning hours of Saturday. Lillie promptly sought out Horace Logan to advise him that Hank was truly sick, couldn't make the Hayride that night, and she was taking him home to Montgomery for a rest during the holidays. Logan had no choice but to grant Hank a leave of absence, reminding Lillie that he was paying Hank enough money to enable him to fly back in order to fulfill his obligations. Soon the three of them, Hank and Lillie and Billie Jean, were piling into the car for the long haul across Louisiana and Mississippi and on into Montgomery. There was no way Hank could drink under those conditions, of course, but his mind was swirling with contradictions. He had left behind a maddening trail of mixed signals—that he was done with the Hayride and headed back to the Opry; that he was going to take a cure in the Caribbean; that he was going to divorce Billie Jean; that he'd found another farm to buy in Franklin; even that he and Audrey might get back together—but the only thing anybody knew for sure was that he had two big shows booked for the holidays: at seven o'clock on New Year's Eve in Charleston, West Virginia, and a two o'clock matinee in Canton, Ohio, on New Year's Day.

It was no picnic for Billie Jean, being holed up with Hank

in his bedroom at Lillie's place. The two women had been speaking to each other only to be civil ever since Lillie learned that Billie Jean had talked Hank out of lending his mother money to buy yet another boardinghouse (she already had two, and Bobbie Jett was stashed at the other, riding out her pregnancy). Hank was in terrible shape, weakened by the flu and his recent bouts with the bottle and the painkillers he was taking for his aching back, and between visits from old friends like Braxton Schuffert (to whom he boasted he was booked up solid until May) he was trying with little success to sleep, often flopped on top of the sheets with his clothes on. This wasn't Billie Jean's town, and there was little she could do except make a run to a drugstore to pick up another prescription for chloral hydrate ordered up by Toby Marshall after a phone call from Lillie. They did make the rounds one night, when Hank got drunk, took to dancing on the counter, and hit Billie Jean in the face when she tried to make him stop. (Obviously, she struck back; Hank is bruised about the head in nearly every snapshot from the final months of the year, dating back to the day of the wedding ceremonies in New Orleans.) Through all of this, Hank managed to slip away long enough to pay a doctor in advance for the delivery of Bobbie Jett's child and to leave fifty dollars for expenses with the cousin, Marie Harvell, who ran the boardinghouse where Bobbie was staying.

When he and Billie Jean got into the convertible for a run down to Georgiana, it was almost as if Hank had a premonition that his days were numbered, that he was running out of time to say some last farewells. They visited his aunt and uncle, Erleen and Taft Skipper, who ran a country store, spending a couple of nights with them. Billie Jean made a strong impression on Hank's kin, not only with her fresh beauty but with her willingness to help cook and wash dishes afterward (Audrey, whenever she had come around, seldom even got out of the car), and at one point Hank sang for them a song he had been carrying around for some time, "The Log Train," a tribute to his father's days in the lumber camps. He decided he wanted to see Lon on Christmas Day, so he and Billie Jean drove up to McWilliams that morning. Nobody was home when they got there—there was no way to call ahead, since Lon didn't have a phone—and when Hank learned they had gone to Selma for the day he left a note and a gift-wrapped five-pound box of candy on the porch. (Lon was so heartbroken after his son's death that he saved the note and wrapping paper for years.) Hank and Billie Jean then drove up to Pine Apple, across the highway from Greenville, and had dinner with Lon's sister Bertha before returning to Montgomery that night. They had tickets for Saturday's Blue-Gray Game, an annual college football all-star exhibition, but it was a cold and windy day so they left before halftime. The next night, Sunday the twenty-eighth, marked the very last time Hank Williams would perform in public. It could hardly be called a concert—more like singing for his supper—when he appeared as a guest at the annual holiday party of the American Federation of Musicians' local, at the Elite Café ("Where the Elite Meet to Eat") in downtown Montgomery. When he had finished his steak, Hank, in a dark blue business suit, slung a guitar over his shoulder, stood in front of a microphone at the head table, and sang four of his songs: "Jambalaya," "Cold, Cold Heart," "You Win Again," and "Lovesick Blues." The 130 members and guests, though primarily involved in jazz and classical and pop music, and not knowing or caring that much for country, gave him a big hand.

. . .

Needing a driver for the long haul to West Virginia and Ohio for the holiday shows, but finding that old buddies like Schuffert were tied to day jobs, Hank had settled on the teenaged son of a friend who owned a local taxi company. Charles Carr had just turned eighteen, was a freshman at Alabama Polytechnic Institute (now Auburn University), had chauffeured Hank before, and could use the $400 to finance the entire coming term. Hank was dressed and ready to go when Carr showed up at the boardinghouse shortly after noon on December 30—crisp blue serge suit, white fedora and cowboy boots, a navy blue overcoat—and the two of them loaded up the trunk of the big-finned powder-blue Cadillac convertible with the things he would need: guitar and stage costumes, a change of clothes, songbooks and photos and records for sale. Billie Jean was there, still offering to accompany Hank on the trip, but it was finally settled that she would fly home to Shreveport and he would call her when he returned to Montgomery. It seemed to Carr that they would never get onto the open road. First they stopped to pick up a six-pack of Falstaff beer to keep Hank company, and when Hank spotted a friend in the parking lot of a diner, a saxophone player named Leo Hudson, who had been at the AMF banquet at the Elite, he insisted Carr stop while they chatted for more than an hour. (Quite unknown to Hank, a worried Lillie was on the phone to Toby Marshall in Oklahoma City, getting him to agree to fly to Charleston and stick with Hank until he got back to Montgomery.) At about 3:30 in the afternoon, under dark and ominous skies, with rain turning to sleet, they finally got onto Highway 31, headed north to Birmingham.

Although the unlikely pair made jovial travel companions—

Carr said he couldn't make any sense out of the Cajun patois in "Jambalaya," and Hank, riding shotgun beside him, merely shrugged and began singing a cappella Red Foley's dark "Midnight"—the trip seemed to be cursed. It was dark when they reached Birmingham. Looking for the Tutwiler Hotel, Birmingham's finest, Carr was stopped by a cop for making an illegal U-turn and told to move on. They settled for lesser digs at the Redmont, dreaming of dinner and bedtime, but within minutes of checking in they were found by two randy female fans who spent a couple of hours cavorting between Hank's and Carr's rooms. They were late getting away the next morning after breakfast at the hotel—only a hundred miles covered from Montgomery to Birmingham, with 580 miles still to go to Charleston, a near-impossible day's drive in good weather to make it by seven o'clock—and here it was New Year's Eve with winter storms sweeping the South. They stopped in Fort Payne, Alabama, for a shave (and a pint of whiskey for Hank), and then they lunched at Chattanooga, where Hank punched Tony Bennett's version of "Cold, Cold Heart" on the jukebox before buying sandwiches and then leaving a fifty-dollar tip for a waiter who reverently called him "Mr. Williams." Then they were off again, and now there was a serious storm in progress. When they got to Knoxville they knew they would never make it to Charleston unless they flew. With snow blanketing the southern Appalachians, they got on a plane at the Knoxville airport at 3:30 in the afternoon, bound for Charleston, but after trying to poke through the blizzard the pilot turned around and returned to Knoxville. Nighttime had fallen in the Smoky Mountains. Hank was worn out, partly from the beer and nips of bourbon and the residue of alcohol that by now was nearly always present in his system, and he and Carr arrived at the Andrew Johnson Hotel at seven o'clock, about the time the show would have been opening in Charleston. Two porters had to assist Hank to the room they shared.

The teenaged driver now had a genuine crisis on his hands. They were more than five hundred miles from Canton, up in northern Ohio, and he assumed the weather was much the same between there and Knoxville. The first thing he did was order two steaks from room service, and Hank took only a few bites before going to sleep, finally rolling off the bed and falling onto the floor. When Hank began hiccuping, sending his body into convulsions, Carr's call to the front desk summoned a doctor, who came to the room and injected two shots, one of vitamin B_6 and one of B_{12}. Then Carr managed to contact the promoter, one A.V. Bamford, who told him the Charleston show had been canceled and strongly advised that they get back into the car and continue driving to Canton; the two o'clock matinee was a sellout, four thousand tickets already sold at $2.50 each, and if Hank didn't make it he would owe $1,000 on a penalty clause. The doctor who had given Hank the vitamin shots said he was okay to travel, so at 10:30 a porter came to the room with a wheelchair, sat Hank in it, and delivered him to the car. Hank managed to get out of the wheelchair and crawl into the backseat without anyone's help, cuddling up with the blanket Carr wrapped around him, and off they lurched into the storm.

Leaning forward in the driver's seat, peering into the mixture of snow and sleet, Carr hadn't driven twenty miles up Highway 11 West before he nearly crashed head-on into a Tennessee patrol car while trying to pass a bus, and had to follow the trooper into the town of Rutledge to pay a seventy-five-dollar fine to a justice of the peace. The trooper asked who was in the backseat and was he all right; Carr told him it was Hank Williams, he was okay, just sleeping off a beer. Forging ahead, dog-tired, Carr stopped to gas up in Bristol, on the Tennessee-Virginia line. There was an all-night diner across the highway, next to a cab stand, and he got the idea to grab something to eat and look for a relief driver to help him. "You want something to eat?" he asked Hank, who had gotten out of the car to stretch, and Hank said all he wanted to do was sleep. It was approaching midnight when Carr was directed to the diner and found a cabdriver who had just finished his shift, one Donald Surface, and he hired him on the spot. Carr couldn't sleep, not with a stranger at the wheel of a car carrying such valuable cargo, but at least he was able to relieve the tension of driving. A couple of hours later, past one o'clock in the morning, he paid Surface twenty-five dollars and let him out at Bluefield, the first town in West Virginia. The snow and sleet had stopped and now, with little more than three hundred miles to go, Canton seemed doable. Carr felt a certain elation as he got back behind the wheel: the traffic was light, nothing but open road lay ahead, the Cadillac's heater and radio were in working order, Hank was finally asleep in the backseat, and he could relax. With luck, they could make it by daybreak. He was looking forward to the afternoon show in Canton, where Hank would be the headliner.

The last time he had seen Hank move and heard him speak was at the service station back in Bristol just before midnight, when Hank said all he wanted to do was sleep and promptly crawled back into the backseat, and Carr presumed Hank was in a deep sleep as the two-lane highway twisted away from Bluefield, tires humming, telephone poles zipping past in the glare of the headlights. He happened to look over his shoulder for a glance at the form in the backseat—Hank was stretched out on his back, his hands folded across his chest, nothing unusual—and when he noticed that the blanket had fallen away he reached over with his right hand, still driving with his left, to fumble for the blanket and cover Hank with it. It was then that he inadvertently touched Hank's hand. It was stone cold. Terror hung in Carr's throat. This was more than he could handle alone. He needed help. Seeing a sign reading "Oak Hill 6," his heart pumping furiously, he floored the Cadillac. At the edge of the tiny town there was a cut-rate gas station. He brought the car to a screeching stop, rushed inside the station, and asked the old man on duty if he would come take a look at the fellow in the backseat. "Looks like you've got a problem," the man drawled after he had done so, and directed Carr to the Oak Hill Hospital. There, he parked around back, walked into the hospital, and asked two interns to come out and check on his passenger. They followed him to the car and needed only a glance at Hank's rigid body. "He's dead, all right," one of them said. "But isn't there something you can do to revive him?" said Carr. "It's too late," he was told. "The man's dead."

The interns hoisted the lifeless body from the backseat of the Cadillac, one holding it by the armpits and the other by the booted feet, and laid it out on a stainless-steel table inside the emergency room. While a doctor was being summoned, Carr went to a phone in the lobby of the hospital to call his father in Montgomery with the news. Just before daybreak, an intern officially pronounced Hank Williams dead, guessing that he might have actually expired around one o'clock in the morning on that New Year's Day. Carr was exhausted and understandably distraught, but the police who had arrived wrote down that he seemed "nervous," and when they noted that Hank's head was bruised they rushed to a judgment that foul play might be involved. Soon the body was being moved to Tyree Funeral Home, across from the hospital, where an autopsy was performed by a doctor who had been called in from the larger hospital in Beckley, a Russian barely fluent in English. Blood samples were put in a bottle, some internal organs in a package, and the state trooper who was directed to rush them to a lab in Charleston for analysis vomited at the sight. The doctor almost casually noted that there were needle marks on the arms and that Hank had recently been severely beaten and kicked in the groin. No drugs were found in the blood, just traces of alcohol. A coroner's jury later confirmed that Hank died of "a severe heart condition and hemorrhage," and let it go at that.

So much for small-town police work and medical attention in the southern outback, in that time and during the early-morning hours of a holiday. Had they fully understood who they were dealing with, had any inkling of the repercussions Hank Williams's passing would bring, they surely would have been more thorough about the autopsy. Needle marks? A "trace" of alcohol, but no mention of the deadly chloral hydrate? Evidence of a recent beating? Carr was "nervous"? Precisely when did Hank die? The police and medical personnel left enough half-answered questions to allow the most spurious rumors to fester after the death. It's quite possible that Hank Williams had almost literally died of a broken heart, that his frail body had simply given out, but suspicions about what *really* happened that night would still be rattling around a half century later. Hundreds of songs would be written about Hank, dozens of them focusing on the night he died. Smarting from the early implications that he might be a suspect, Carr would go years before he would talk about it; and even then he would complain, with reason, that people kept getting it wrong. The legend quickly outgrew the vague facts.

As the sun rose over the Blue Ridge on New Year's Day and word spread of Hank's death, there was a swirl of activity. Lillie dispatched a telegram to her daughter, Irene—"Come at once Hank is dead"—and then called Charles Carr in Oak Hill to say, "Don't let anything happen to the car." Billie Jean began screaming and crying when she heard, but soon she was calling Carr with the same message about the car. Audrey had been partying on New Year's Eve with the wife of the promoter, A. V. Bamford, at a posh club in Nashville, and the fate of the powder-blue Cadillac was on her mind as well. Carr dutifully drove the car to the Pure Oil station in Oak Hill, where it was briefly impounded before being moved to the local Ford dealership, and then he tried to catch a couple of hours' sleep in a suite at the funeral home. He had become something of a star-crossed celebrity in Oak Hill, the teenaged driver at the center of this terrible tragedy, and sympathetic townsfolk did their best to soften his grief: "An important man in town was throwing a New Year's Day buffet at his house, and I was invited. They were really nice people, everybody was, and I was treated like a king. I even watched some of the bowl games on television."

Meanwhile, in Canton, Ohio, the realization that Hank had really died this time was setting in. Many of the principals—

entertainers, promoters, even the quack doctor Toby Marshall—
had shown up in Charleston only to find that the New Year's
Eve show had been canceled due to bad weather and had
driven through the night to Canton. When they arrived at the
auditorium in the late morning to set up for the two o'clock
show, they were met at the door by Bamford, who broke the
news. Few took it harder than Don Helms, the steel guitarist,
who had been Hank's best friend since 1944. There was a full
house of four thousand paying customers in the auditorium
when the emcee, an Akron disc jockey, stepped to the microphone. "This morning," he said, "on his way to Canton to do
this show, Hank Williams died in his car." There were some
sprinkles of laughter in the audience, from people who had
heard many excuses for his no-shows in recent years. "This is
no joke, ladies and gentlemen," he continued. "Hank Williams
is dead." Now there was open weeping, even crying from the
cast members behind the curtain, and the lights were dimmed
and a spotlight was thrown in a circle on the stage where Hank
might have been standing, and then the audience heard the
cries of Don Helms's steel guitar playing the opening bars of "I
Saw the Light."

And then the vultures came. First to arrive in Oak Hill was
Lillie, who had flown up from Montgomery with Charles Carr's
father—when the Charleston airport was still fogged in, they
had to fly to Roanoke, Virginia, and hire a cab for the perilous
three-hour drive over the mountains to Oak Hill—and she
promptly commandeered the Cadillac and Hank's belongings:
costumes, boots, guitars, jewelry, money, even his wedding
ring. Somebody had already made off with his white fedora and
a pistol. When Billie Jean, the grieving young widow, arrived

from Shreveport with her father, a police sergeant, there was nothing they could do but fly back home and await the funeral. Audrey didn't make it, but already she and Lillie were bonding in an unlikely conspiracy against Billie Jean in a power struggle that was sure to evolve over Hank's remains; most important, over the staggering onrush of money about to pile up in royalties from his songs. Toby Marshall drove a rental car down from Canton and had the audacity to present Lillie and then Billie Jean a bill of $736.39 for "services rendered," which each in her outrage threw back in his face. Hank had left no will, which meant Lon would be designated as executor of the estate, but when Lillie filled out the death certificate in Oak Hill she listed the father as "deceased."

Late on the afternoon of January 2, 1953, following a hearse holding Hank's body dressed in a white stage outfit, the powder-blue Cadillac convertible, with Charles Carr and his father in front and Lillie and the shameless "doctor" Toby Marshall in the rear, began the long overnight drive back home to Montgomery. Oncoming truckers, taking a guess, tapped their air horns in salute. It was reminiscent of the mournful last rides home of two other recent American icons, when distraught citizens had lined the railroad tracks for hundreds of miles as the bodies of President Franklin Delano Roosevelt and Jimmie Rodgers, "the Singing Brakeman," were towed to rest. It rained almost all the way as the tandem made its way southward, tracing the route Hank and Carr had made days earlier during the storms, and whenever they pulled in for gas or eats people crowded around the hearse with its West Virginia license tags. "Hank in there?" they would ask, for there had been great outpourings of grief all over the country since the news, almost as if a head of state had died, and they couldn't keep themselves from trying to peer through the drawn curtains for one final look at the greatest man who ever sang a country song.

The first weekend of the new year, 1953, broke cold and bright over Lillie's boardinghouse in Montgomery, which became the center of everything. Hank's body lay in state there (after morticians, per Lillie's request, had to get back into the coffin and break the ankles so he could be buried with his boots on), to be viewed by the dozens of family and friends rushing in for the funeral service on Sunday at the city auditorium. Fred and Wesley Rose drove down from Nashville to serve as pallbearers, and a dozen stars of the Opry were flown in on a charter to perform at the public ceremony along with the Drifting Cowboys. Then came the clamorous arrivals of the two wives, Audrey and Billie Jean, creating a madness of its own in the close quarters of the cramped two-story frame house on South McDonough Street: after a frantic scramble to find what scribbled lyrics Hank might have left behind, a treasure hunt involving Audrey and Billie Jean and Lillie and sister Irene, a sheaf of them was found by Lillie in Billie Jean's bedroom while she was in the bathroom and was eventually turned over to Fred Rose. The "deceased" Lon Williams, still hurting from having missed Hank's impromptu visit a week earlier, had five dollars in his pocket when he arrived, having hitched a ride in from McWilliams—uninvited to his son's funeral—and spent it all on a bouquet of flowers. There, at the boardinghouse, he and Lillie had it out over who would become executor of Hank's estate, and he caved in: if that's what it would take to finally get her out of his life, he said, she could have it. Meanwhile, in another of Lillie's boardinghouses across town, the pregnancy of Bobbie Jett was nearing fruition.

On Sunday, Hank's funeral became the biggest spectacle to hit Montgomery since the inauguration of Jefferson Davis as president of the Confederacy on the steps of the Alabama state capitol in 1861. Some twenty thousand people milled around outside the auditorium, fewer than three thousand of them allowed inside to view the body in its open casket (about two hundred blacks crowded the balcony). Fitfully seated in the front rows were the three dueling women, wearing black and openly wailing, and on the stage were the Drifting Cowboys and the Opry stars and even a black quartet known as the Southwind Singers. It was all Don Helms could do to contain himself as he played his mournful steel guitar from the stage, looking down at Hank's stone corpse in the casket below, while Roy Acuff and Ernest Tubb and Red Foley sang their goodbyes: "I Saw the Light" and "Beyond the Sunset" and "Peace in the Valley." The preacher opened his remarks by saying that Hank Williams had "just answered the call of the last roundup." And they trekked off to witness Hank's burial in a hillside cemetery in the shadow of the capitol, beneath an ornate headstone featuring a forlorn, carved cowboy hat.

Better Dead than Alive

During his lifetime, there were only four mentions of Hank Williams in the Nashville newspapers. That was partly because the *Banner* and the *Tennessean* more or less left the Opry and the burgeoning music business to their own devices in those days—it was only "hillbilly" music, after all, something the pooh-bahs of the "Athens of the South" still held with contempt—but there was more to it than that. Only three years and seven months had passed between his debut on the Opry and his death, at the age of twenty-nine, and it was as though he had come and gone so quickly, like an unidentified comet streaking through the night sky, that the sheer power of Hank's coming had barely sunk in on the city. Even the people in the industry seemed slow to pick up on it. There were the anticipated expressions of homage from the music-makers in town ("We'll never see his likes again," said Jim Denny of the Opry), while a few dared to agree with Jerry Byrd, the steel guitarist who had suffered Hank's inconsistencies: "He did as much to hurt country music as he did to help it." It wasn't until reports began pouring in from the American outback, from Cajun shacks in the Louisiana swamps to mining towns in Appalachia to migrant workers' camps in the San Joaquin Valley, that the idea began to register: the working classes had lost their poet, a proletarian prophet who had touched their souls with his simple heartbreaking lyrics. A traveling salesman out

of Atlanta remembered stopping at a diner near Bristol on that
New Year's morning and seeing his waitress fall apart at the
news as she was pouring his coffee; a memory that led him to
begin work on a play about Hank, fifty years later.

That was Hank's true audience, the waitresses and the
route salesmen and the farmers and the truck drivers of the
world, and they began to be heard from almost immediately in
their clamor to buy his records in the aftermath of his passing.
"The marketing of the Hank Williams legend began with Wesley and Fred Rose on the drive to Montgomery for the funeral,"
said Hugh Cherry, an influential country disc jockey at the
time. The Roses and MGM had gone into overdrive to produce
Hank's last recordings, and four in a row reached the top of
Billboard's country charts; the first being "I'll Never Get Out
of This World Alive," a humorous novelty belying its ominous
title. Of his ten No.1 records, four of them came in the six
months following his death. The people had voted, but the industry would lag behind for years that stretched into decades.
It wasn't until 1961 that Hank, along with Fred Rose and Jimmie Rodgers, was elected as a charter member of the new
Country Music Hall of Fame. His home state of Alabama was
even slower to grant recognition; a statue of Hank didn't go up
in Montgomery until 1991, and the state finally got around to
honoring him in '97 by designating a thirteen-mile stretch
along I-65 between the Greenville and Georgiana exits as
Hank's "Lost Highway." There were a lot of self-serving memoirs printed as booklets or pamphlets, by family members or
fans or fellow musicians, but the first bona fide hardcover book
by a knowledgeable independent writer wasn't published until
1970. The world is still waiting for a definitive movie about
Hank's life; the one attempt, *Your Cheatin' Heart,* of 1964,

turning out to be an almost comical fantasy starring a bronzed playboy Hollywood actor named George Hamilton and authorized by Audrey, who made of herself a tragic heroine and allowed no mention of Billie Jean Jones in the script.

There were signs toward the end that Hank himself seemed to believe he might be better off dead than alive, and some of those closest to him surely felt that way when he actually took his leave. He had certainly stretched the patience of the people in the business—promoters like Oscar Davis, fellow musicians like Byrd, executives like the Opry's Denny, even the devoted record producer and surrogate father Fred Rose—but none had paid such prices as Lillie and Audrey. From the very instant of Hank's death, those two formed an alliance to make sure they got what they figured they had coming. Hank had left behind a gold mine, especially with the portfolio of songs he had written, and it promised to increase as the years passed and his legend grew to almost mythical proportions. Lillie had devoted twenty-nine hard years to nurturing her son, for better or for worse, Audrey nine, and few would contest that they were the rightful heirs to the fortune. The first thing they did after the burial was to box out Billie Jean, who had put in only three months as his bride, coercing her into accepting a $30,000 payoff to give up any future rights as Hank's widow. (For a brief period, there were two "Mrs. Hank Williamses" working the road, Audrey and Billie Jean, but the buyout quickly ended that maudlin chapter.) As for the baby girl delivered by Bobbie Jett two days after Hank's burial, Lillie obeyed the papers Hank and Bobbie had signed: she adopted the child and sent Bobbie on her way, ultimately to California, never to be heard from again.

Hank's name stayed in the news for the next couple of

years. Two weeks after the burial, wild rumors began in Montgomery when passersby saw workmen digging up Hank's coffin and moving it by lantern light in the middle of the night, but as it turned out Lillie had simply bought a newer and bigger space as the family plot. In March, when Toby Marshall's wife died of mysterious circumstances, he was hauled into court; the ensuing investigation and hearings led to a side trip into Marshall's part in Hank's death, the bogus doctor being so bold as to claim it was a suicide, but the only thing they could nail him on was a parole violation. As MGM released new recordings, each of them zooming to the top of the charts, Hank's worth was increasing month by month, filling Audrey's bank account. Soon she became quite the party animal, insinuating herself wherever there were gatherings of music moguls and pickers and up-and-coming wannabe singers (who all understood that marriage was out of the question as long as she remained the single, grieving widow), and the first signs were appearing of her overuse of the drugs and the booze that ultimately would do her in. Hank was, indeed, of more value to her dead than alive. Hank, Jr., only three years old at the time of his daddy's death, had to have it explained to him who these people were parking on the street and brazenly trying to peek into the windows of the house on Franklin Road at all hours. Reports came from Montgomery of fans flocking to the cemetery, leaving flowers and even bottles of whiskey at the new gravesite. When Fred Rose died of a heart attack in December of '54, and Lillie died in her sleep in February of '55, it was as though only then had Hank finally passed.

And then, when a teenager named Elvis Presley came out with his first record in the summer of 1955, a new question arose:

Had he lived, would Hank have been able to survive Elvis? An entirely new generation had arrived in America, the baby boomers, kids born at the end of the Second World War, and as they neared their teen years it became evident that country music was their parents' music, not theirs. Relatively affluent, facing a promising new world free of war and economic depression, they were looking for something fresh that they could call their own. The grandfatherly president, retired general Dwight Eisenhower, wasn't it, nor was Hank Williams. The dead Hank was to them just another old fart whose time had passed, a drunken hillbilly who whined about "pitchers from life's other side" and cheating hearts and being so lonesome he could cry. They much preferred this new guy, Elvis, with his pegged trousers and pompadour hairdo and a sneer on his lips and a sensuous wiggle to his hips. They loved the anarchistic thrust of his music because, if for no other reason, it pissed off their parents. Elvis was a threat; Hank was passé.

The coming of Elvis and rock 'n' roll nearly swamped country music. The number of full-time country radio stations plummeted, many of the faithful outlets like WCKY and even the Mexican border stations abandoning Hank for Elvis, and almost overnight the glory years of country music in the late forties and early fifties became history. The party was over for Ernest Tubb and Webb Pierce and Lefty Frizzell and the other great roadhouse troubadours of their time—the only ones who survived were performers like Johnny Cash, for instance, country "rockabillies" from the tag end of the era who could meet Elvis's new sound halfway—and soon, by the sixties, country music as it once had been known could be found only on "golden oldies" radio portions or the all-night truckers' shows or, God bless it, the Grand Ole Opry. Late in that

decade, with rock 'n' roll flying high, producers like Chet
Atkins, a technical whiz who had sometimes backed Hank on
guitar, responded with something called "the Nashville
sound": at once simple but slick, soothing pop music with a
steel guitar and a *y'all* behind it, using echo chambers and full
string sections recruited from the Nashville Symphony. New
releases of Hank's tunes, either heavily orchestrated overdubs
or new cuts by pop singers, were thin imitations that pleased
neither the rock 'n' roll kids nor the old-timers.

Even Hank's own son eventually turned against his daddy's
music, if only as a matter of personal survival. Hank, Jr., was
cursed by the name from the start, and his mother made things
worse even while the boy was still tooling around Nashville in
the convertible in which his father had died. Audrey was calling every shot in the poor kid's life, forcing Hank's music on
him—she booked him for his debut at fourteen in the auditorium at Canton, Ohio, on the anniversary of the concert Hank
never made—and for a while he put on an eerie act: the house
lights would go down, an image of Hank, Sr., would appear on
a screen, and Junior, in a spangled white cowboy suit, would
sing a medley of "songs my daddy left me." (The most chilling
of all came in the late eighties when a lost demo was found of
Hank's "There's a Tear in My Beer," the ultimate drinking
song, and technology enabled father and son to sing it "together" on a video.) The boy was himself screwed up on drugs
and booze, fighting this career foisted on him all the way, until
at twenty he nearly died in a mountain-climbing accident and
determined, while laid up in the hospital, that he was going to
become his own man. Thus was born the Hank, Jr., who survived: a bearded, dope-smoking, hell-raising biker of a good
old boy who attracted a frightening following of similar types

who rolled in on their Harleys draped in Confederate flags. "I don't have to do this to make a living, you know," he liked to tell his fans at concerts nearly fifty years after his father's death. "Every month I get a check for forty thousand dollars from songs my daddy wrote."

He would have been getting twice that from royalties had things gone differently for the baby born two days after Hank's burial. Bobbie Jett had named her daughter Antha Belle Jett, giving up all rights and leaving the scene as per agreement with Hank, but a month later, when the girl was adopted by Lillie, she was renamed Cathy Yvonne (from "Jambalaya") Stone. When Lillie died in 1955, she was adopted again, this time by a couple in Mobile who named her Catherine Louise Deupree. All records were sealed and Cathy was about to graduate from the University of Alabama, doing just fine and blissfully unaware of her heritage, until the day she turned twenty-one, in 1974, when she was notified that a check for $2,000 from the estate of a Mrs. Stone was being held for her in Montgomery. She spent the next fifteen years uncovering the secrets of her life, and finally in the late eighties she and her new lawyer-husband managed to satisfy the courts that she was, indeed, the illegitimate daughter of Hank Williams, Sr. This time she renamed herself, and soon she was touring as "Jett Williams," singing her daddy's songs and sharing his royalties with her dear half brother; creating yet another cut of the pie, Billie Jean having won a court decision when copyrights came up for renewal in the mid-seventies. Neither Hank, Jr., nor his own son, Hank III, a punk-rocking wraith with a remarkable physical resemblance to his wasted grandfather, was amused. But that was it, as far as anybody knew, the end of the line of succession.

The question of whether Hank would have weathered the coming of Elvis, had he lived to see it, is a moot point, hinging on the wildest conjecture. He had shown some signs in his last year or two of composing tunes that would meet the new criteria—"Kaw-liga" and "Jambalaya" were, after all, light entertainments with a catchy beat—but at heart a Hank Williams song depended on themes drawn from despair and disappointment. Young Hiram was a child of the Depression and the war years, when everybody was suffering, and his music reflected that. America had gotten enough of all that when the fifties arrived, with its newfound muscle and hope for a brighter future, and the time had come to celebrate. "Jailhouse Rock" and "Blue Suede Shoes," noisy blatherings whose bouncy lyrics were beside the point, fit the bill. Had Hank miraculously survived to compete against Elvis and the waves of other rock-and-rollers, we can only guess whether he might have succeeded. The odds say no. He was too much a poet for his particular time, and that time had passed. His death while at the top of his game was, as the saying goes, a good career move.

Throughout the decades since, the coming of a new year had always brought a special chill to the millions of his fans around the world. Charles Carr, who grew up to become a successful dealer in real estate, had learned to leave his cell phone connected in Montgomery as the clock ticked toward midnight on New Year's Eve, waiting for the calls sure to come from people who just wanted to talk to him about that surreal night of the snowstorms when Hank passed away in the backseat of the Cadillac, and he took a record number of them on the last day of 2002. Marking the fiftieth anniversary of Hank's death, the year 2003 would see an outpouring of commemora-

tions and reexaminations of the life and music of the man who
was, to most fans of a certain age, the only country singer and
songwriter who ever really counted. It promised to be a busy
year not only for Hank's son and daughter and grandson (no
other members of the immediate family survive, including Audrey, who died in 1975) but everybody else with the most tenuous connections to the legend: Drifting Cowboys, natives of
south Alabama, Nashville musicians, even the handful of
Hank impersonators roaming the land. Just released were a
photo album and an expensive boxed set of every recording
Hank left behind; coming up were paperback reissues of some
of the Hank biographies; Hank, Jr., and Hank III would host
the televised portion of the Opry on the first Saturday night of
the year (a special guest being Rufus "Tee-Tot" Payne's
eighty-two-year-old son); and cable TV's Country Music Television was releasing another documentary on Hank's life and
times. In the spring, a musical entitled *Hank Williams: Lost
Highway* was to open Off Broadway in Manhattan.

The year was kicked off shortly after dawn on the first day
of January at the Williams family plot in Montgomery, on the
hill adjacent to the Alabama state capitol building. Buried beside Hank's soaring marble tomb are Audrey and Lillie (Lon,
who outlived Lillie by fifteen years, is buried in McWilliams).
It was, someone said, "Hank's kind of day"—bleak, overcast,
windy—and some 250 fans from as far away as Massachusetts
and Germany huddled around the headstones to hear a few
words from the son of the preacher who had conducted the funeral services for Hank at the Montgomery auditorium fifty
years earlier. Charles Carr was there, of course, along with a
few of the surviving Drifting Cowboys. Absent were Hank, Jr.,
and, more pointedly, Jett Williams, ever the outsider. "Is it his

daughter, or is it not?" said Hank's half sister, Leila Griffin, echoing persistent doubts held by a remarkable number of family and friends in spite of the facts of Jett's lineage. Afterward they trundled off to the Hank Williams Museum downtown, which is dominated by the powder-blue Cadillac convertible, for hot coffee and plates brimming with black-eyed peas and corn bread, and soon a sort of hootenanny broke out: Don Helms began playing Hank's greatest hits, and aging fans who had brought along their guitars were scrambling to join the greatest Cowboy of them all to play and sing along and shed a tear or two in memory of their long-fallen hero. When dark had fallen over the city, scores of the "mourners" gathered in the cold mist around the bronze statue of Hank down the street from the museum, holding candles and singing "I Saw the Light."

On the first weekend in June of every year, a Hank Williams Festival is held in Georgiana, on the grounds of the restored white frame house where young Hiram spent his childhood, and this one in 2003 was special because it marked the fiftieth anniversary of the man's death. Torrential rains held the crowd to some two thousand, lugging coolers and lawn chairs, their fervor nevertheless running as deep as the quagmire formed by the relentless rain. The nearest motels in Greenville were fully booked, but the true believers came piling into Georgiana in pickups and campers, bearing tags and bumper stickers reading *Gone Hankin'*, crowding into yards and vacant lots to form little bivouacs whence came yodels and rebel yells and sing-alongs and smoke from campfires not unlike the encampments found at stock-car tracks on NASCAR weekends. It was a pilgrimage, pure and simple, some of the fans having come from Europe and Asia, and the incessant rain and the noisy passage of trains through their midst lent an eerie air to the celebration. It was all Hank, all the time, on a stage fronting an acre of land paved with asphalt and covered by a steel roof: the presentation of "Miss Hank Williams and Her Court," Hank songs from some faded Nashville performers, appearances by the last of the Drifting Cowboys, a word from the president of the Hank Williams Fan Club (who maintains a spare bed in her house in case Hank shows up and "needs a place to rest"), and an hour-long show of Hank's greatest hits by an impersonator from Ohio who turned out to be not at all bad in spite of his shoulder-length hair. Finally, at prime time on Saturday night, out pranced Jett Williams in a white outfit, singing "Jambalaya" to the accompaniment of "Uncle Don" Helms on the steel guitar, and she was greeted as one of the family until she called for quiet so she could dedicate a song to "my friend, my lover, my husband, my lawyer . . . without whom there would be no Jett Williams." Hank, Jr., and Hank III had let them down by abandoning the music, and there were still a lot of the most fervent fans who didn't want to believe the story of Hank's long-lost daughter. They certainly weren't prepared to hear her serenade the lawyer who had made it all possible, Keith Adkinson, and with a sensuous pop song like "Make Love to Me" at that. To them, it was like breaking wind in church. As the festival wound down that night, with fans queuing up at tables to get their CDs and photos and programs signed by the entertainers, the lines were longest for Don Helms, not Jett Williams. Forget, hell.

Although he liked Jett and worked about two dozen shows a year with her, Helms understood how the fans felt. "I'm their connection to Hank," he was saying one steamy morning in

August of a year dedicated to memorializing Hank's death. "I played for Hank, Jr., for a while at first, but when his music changed my steel wasn't quite right. 'Tricephus,' now"—his playful nickname for the son of "Bocephus"—"forget it. But when I'm playing steel for Jett and she's singing all of her daddy's songs I might as well be playing with Hank. When they hear me, they feel like they're hearing Hank." Helms had just turned seventy-six, but he was staying busy: working the road with Jett, doing about a dozen of his own concerts every year, and putting in a star appearance at the annual convention of steel guitarists in St. Louis. He never failed to bring tears during his concerts: "I'll get choked and teary-eyed, myself, when the crowd is good, it's warm, and the music's right. They'll turn the lights down and I'll say, 'Close your eyes and think of Hank,' and when I start in on 'Cold, Cold Heart' people get to crying. Me, too. I hope I never lose that feeling."

He was in the den of his house in Hendersonville, a town north of Nashville where most of the country musicians once lived, a rambling brick ranch house he and his wife, Hazel, had occupied since the fifties. He and Hazel had been married "forever"—they went back with Hank and Audrey to their courtship days in Andalusia during the Second World War—raised their children there, and now he didn't go anywhere without her. There was barely a surface in the house not covered by a piece of needlework fashioned by Hazel, and she was in the living room, knitting some more, while he sat at the steel guitar he bought for $100 in '48. (Marty Stuart, the Opry performer who lives nearby and is a prime collector of Hank memorabilia, had made a standing offer of $100,000 for the most famous steel in the music business.) Don was noodling the strings, just messing around, fretting the strains of "Cold,

Cold Heart" and whatever came to mind, thinking back over the years with Hank, both good and bad: picking up the pawn-shop billy clubs they would need if they were going to play roadhouses like Thigpen's Log Cabin, dropping Hank off at the sanitarium's forbidding stone "huts" to dry out, stepping aside as fights broke out between Hank and Audrey, watching the way crowds were mesmerized when Hank bent over the microphone and swayed as he began to sing his sad songs.

"Sometimes I get tired of talking about him," he said. A grand total of ninety musicians were Drifting Cowboys at one time or another, and Helms is about the last one alive and fully in charge of his senses. "Fans come up and ask me what Hank was *really* like and I've gotten to where I'll just say, 'Well, he was skinny, all right.' Everybody's got his own story, anyway, no matter what I say. 'Whatever,' they'll tell me, 'but, see, I was there that night, and I know . . .' Well, I really *was* there for just about all of it. What really worries me the most is that when I'm gone that whole beautiful story will get done wrong. People keep wanting to hear new stories about Hank, but there are no new stories. They'll make him out to be a junkie or a pill-head, but the only thing about Hank and pills was that he overused 'em. Everything he did was bad for his health, that's all." Helms stroked the opening lines to "Your Cheatin' Heart," the most familiar refrain in country music. "He was my fishing buddy, my bowling buddy, my boss, my best friend," he said. "The hardest thing I ever did was stand on the stage at his funeral, looking right down on him in that coffin, and start playing for him. I miss him. He's all I've got."

Epilogue: Legacy

Daddy and I never got to see him in person. The closest we got was on my first trip to the Opry, at the age of sixteen, when we found ourselves among the families milling on the sidewalk out front of the Ryman late on a steamy Saturday afternoon in August of '52. Mama and Sis kept our places in line while Daddy and I mounted the steps to peek at the night's schedule of entertainers, posted on the huge double doors. Listed were the heroes of my youth—Roy Acuff, Little Jimmy Dickens, Minnie Pearl, Hank Snow, Ernest Tubb, Carl Smith—but no Hank Williams. "Guess y'all didn't hear Hank got fired," some old boy told us. *Say it ain't so,* I thought. It was like finally making it to Yankee Stadium only to learn that Babe Ruth wouldn't play that day.

When we got the news that Hank had died, at the beginning of the new year some four months later, it was as though there had been a death in the family. It wasn't that we could personally relate to his lyrics—Daddy was a one-woman man ("It's all I can do to keep up with your mama") and I hadn't yet had a real girlfriend—but we, like any other southerners from the working class, could sense the pain and loneliness expressed in the simplest terms and certainly understood the language. While other boys my age were collecting baseball cards, I was buying every 45-r.p.m. recording Hank ever produced; and Daddy was intensifying his replications of Hank tunes on the piano back home. Music flowed from the open windows of our house, either me playing my Hank records or Daddy banging out "Your Cheatin' Heart" on his piano, and our neighbors later told me of sitting on their front porches, Hank fans or not, enjoying the free entertainment.

Like most Americans my age, I drifted away from the music when I went off to college in the fifties, forsaking Hank for Elvis and rock 'n' roll ("Forgot your raisin', didn't you?" Daddy put it), but I was soon back in the fold. Unhappily married, although for reasons entirely different from Hank's, I was suffering my first defeats and, consequently, when I reached my thirties, found myself being comforted by the sad-ass blues lyrics that Hank had been writing before I fully appreciated them. I had become a writer, as it happened, and in trying to find my voice I turned to two men who were minimalists, masters of understated simplicity: Ernest Hemingway and Hank Williams. My first book was *The Nashville Sound*, the beginning of a portfolio that would be about southerners in various degrees of stress: stock-car drivers, lost girls, minor league ballplayers, drunks, bored teenagers in the Alabama boondocks. (While in Nashville, I asked Chet Atkins if he thought Audrey might talk to me. "You're a handsome young man, so I don't see why not," he said. "Just don't go over there alone and after dark. She's armed and dangerous.") By the late seventies I was a runaway husband and father, living in a dollar-a-day rooming house in Montgomery, only four blocks up the street from Lillie Williams's first boardinghouse on South Perry Street, drunk and suicidal and unable to write, falling apart every time I heard Hank's "My Son Calls Another Man Daddy." Forgotten my raising? Hell, no. I was living it to the hilt, background music provided by Hank Williams.

.   .   .

Daddy, meanwhile, never wavered. When he popped in to visit me in Nashville while I was working on my book there, he was much more interested in seeing Hank's old house on Franklin Road than in meeting any of the new breed of country singers backstage at the Ryman Auditorium. He made his last run as a trucker at the age of seventy-one, in 1982 (personally loading a trailer with 250-pound surplus aircraft tires at an air force base in Texas), complaining about the demise of the all-night truckers' shows on the radio, and then descended into an uneasy retirement. When Mama came down with Alzheimer's and he followed her into a nursing home, he got thrown out and had to move back to the house when he insisted on sitting at the white baby grand in the atrium, frightening the blue-haired widows by playing Hank Williams all day. The last time we spoke was on a day when I visited him, drinking out of lonesomeness, and invited him to check out my new Chevy Blazer. A Chrysler man, he wasn't impressed. "Probably got a bad transmission," he said.

"Yeah, but it's got a real good radio," I told him.

"Will it pick up country music?"

"Of *course* it will."

"Must be a hell of a radio, then," he said. "Ain't been no country music since Hank died."

He had become friends with a fellow named Eddie Burns, host of the live *Country Boy Eddie Show* on WBRC-TV. Every morning at daybreak, Birmingham would awaken to the sounds of Eddie braying like a mule—*Hee-haw, hee-haw*—and then breaking into a hoedown with a house band. Eddie had never met Hank Williams, but never got over seeing him once and loved his music. Daddy had taken to watching the show every morning, over his first shooter of bourbon, and more than once he had put on a coat and tie and driven across town to pop in on the set as an uninvited guest and, much to Mama's chagrin, sit down and bang away on "Lovesick Blues" or some other Hank tune, live and on local television. Eddie had an hour to fill, enjoyed Daddy's company, and didn't seem to mind.

When Daddy died in '88, nearly forty years after that first trip I made with him during the summer of Hank, I chose to spend the night before his burial at the family house, to be alone with my memories of him. I wandered about the house that night, going through scrapbooks and snapshots, running my fingers over the keys of the old piano, and as it turned out I fell asleep on the sofa while a movie was running on WBRC-TV. I was startled awake at daybreak by the braying of Country Boy Eddie and the fiddle tune that introduced the show. Eddie came back after a commercial break, with a somber look on his face: "We've lost a good friend, folks. Y'all remember Paul Hemphill. He could play Hank better'n Hank could. . . ." So that more or less served as my father's obituary notice. Later that day, as they lowered his body into the ground, a preacher had to shout to be heard over the commotion rising from below the hill. Swinging around the cemetery was Interstate 20, crowded with muscular eighteen-wheel semis, headed west, their drivers grabbing gears and jockeying for position and, surely, trying to find some good country music on the radio. I knew they would play hell finding any.

ACKNOWLEDGMENTS

Writing fifty years after Hank's death, when most of the principals are gone, I'm much obliged to those music historians who preceded me, especially Colin Escott. His book *Hank Williams: The Biography* (with George Merritt and William MacEwen) and his illustrated *Snapshots from the Lost Highway* (with Kira Florita) and, most particularly, his and Florita's production of the boxed set *The Complete Hank Williams,* proved invaluable. For the material dealing with Hank and the Carter Family, I'm indebted to Mark Zwonitzer and Charles Hirshberg for their Carter biography, *Will You Miss Me When I'm Gone?* Many thanks go to the archivists at the Country Music Foundation, whose transcribed interviews of people who knew Hank and his times are a treasure. I'm especially grateful for guidance from Don Helms and Marty Stuart and Tom Robinson in Nashville, and for the good people in south Alabama who shared their stories. It goes without saying that being my father's son, a child of Hank's South, informs much of what is written in this book; and it took my agent, Sterling Lord, aging like fine wine, to point that out. Finally, and once again, I embrace my wife, Susan Percy, whose enthusiasm for Hank and his music just goes to show that even Phi Beta Kappas get the blues.